D0216277

King Lear

KING LEAR

A Guide to the Play

JAY L. HALIO

Greenwood Guides to Shakespeare

Greenwood Press
Westport, Connecticut • London

Library of Congress Cataloging-in-Publication Data

Halio, Jay L.
    King Lear : a guide to the play / Jay L. Halio.
      p. cm.—(Greenwood guides to Shakespeare)
    Includes bibliographical references and index.
    ISBN 0–313–31618–X (alk. paper)
    1. Shakespeare, William, 1564–1616. King Lear. 2. Lear, King (Legendary character),
in literature. 3. Fathers and daughters in literature. 4. Kings and rulers in literature. 5.
Tragedy. I. Title. II. Series.
PR2819.H35   2001
822.3'3—dc21   2001023330

British Library Cataloguing in Publication Data is available.

Copyright © 2001 by Jay L. Halio

All rights reserved. No portion of this book may be
reproduced, by any process or technique, without the
express written consent of the publisher.

Library of Congress Catalog Card Number: 2001023330
ISBN: 0–313–31618–X

First published in 2001

Greenwood Press, 88 Post Road West, Westport, CT 06881
An imprint of Greenwood Publishing Group, Inc.
www.greenwood.com

Printed in the United States of America

The paper used in this book complies with the
Permanent Paper Standard issued by the National
Information Standards Organization (Z39.48–1984).

10 9 8 7 6 5 4 3 2 1

To the Students of Three Universities

The University of Delaware
The University of California, Davis
The University of Cyprus

and

To the Participants in the Seminar,
"Shakespeare: Enacting the Text,"
Sponsored by the National Endowment
for the Humanities

CONTENTS

PREFACE

"Criticism risks irrelevance if it evades confronting greatness directly," Harold Bloom says, "and Lear perpetually challenges the limits of criticism."[1] He is here speaking of King Lear, the character, not the play, but elsewhere in his essay he makes it clear that he has the play very much in mind as one of the greatest works of art that Shakespeare—or anyone else—has penned. And so it is. This book is a modest attempt, not to encompass the greatness of *King Lear*, for that defies criticism, but to confront its greatness and describe as many aspects of its nature as possible.

Accordingly, a many-faceted approach is requisite to this endeavor. To begin, one must understand its textual history. That Shakespeare took extraordinary pains in the composition of *King Lear* is apparent from the number and quality of his revisions, first during the initial composition, then later after the play had first been published in the quarto of 1608. While we cannot *prove* that Shakespeare was the reviser, much of the evidence available points in that direction. Hence, the other authoritative text of the play, in the great Folio of 1623, presents a considerably altered version, so that what we have, in effect, is two different plays: *The History of King Lear*, as the quarto was called, and *The Tragedy of King Lear*, as the Folio named it.

While some scholars still maintain that both quarto and Folio represent imperfect representations of a lost Shakespearean original, many today accept this two-text theory. The editors of the Oxford *Complete Works*, for example, print *both* the quarto and Folio versions in their edition. In Taylor and Warren's collection of essays, *The Division of the Kingdoms*, many essays explore the differences between the two texts.[2] Neverthe-less, many extant editions still provide conflated editions of *King Lear*, that is, editions that combine the two versions into one, splicing passages unique to one text into the other, producing a single oversized play that Shakespeare never saw performed or expected to see. Fortunately, most recent conflated editions indicate as clearly as possible what the unique passages are, and, in their collations, show further what the variant read-ings are of single words or phrases.

The second chapter of this book, dealing with sources and contexts of *King Lear*, addresses another fascinating issue. Shakespeare must have been a voracious reader, although we still do not know where he had access to the many volumes scholars have identified as influencing his work. But he certainly knew the story of King Lear and his daughters and the account of the Paphlagonian king and his sons in Sir Philip Sidney's *Arcadia*. As regards minor sources—those that provided slight topical allusions or analogues—he probably picked up many of them from conversations or just listening to friends and colleagues talk. As an actor himself and a man of the theater, he also had acquaintance with a large number of plays, some of which may have influenced his own compositions. Acting companies, such as the King's Men (or the Lord Chamberlain's Men, as it was formerly called), were repertory compa-nies. Plays did not have long runs, as successful dramas, and especially musicals, do on Broadway or the West End in London today. A run of four or five performances was about as much as could be expected. Especially interesting plays were performed at court before the king and his courtiers, as the title page of the quarto of 1608 informs us *King Lear* was performed.

For *King Lear*, Shakespeare determined upon a double plot—two fully developed actions that complement each other: the Lear story, and the Gloucester story. Although they have much in common, they are not simply repetitions of the same situation. Shakespeare apparently wanted to universalize his theme, as many critics contend, by showing that what could happen at one level of society could happen at another, and so on down the line. But he did more: he showed the different ways men like Lear and Gloucester confront their fate. In addition, Shakespeare devel-oped other contrasts, for example, the contrast between Cordelia and Edgar, both of whom serve as ministers to their fathers after catastrophe has struck. But Cordelia is absent during acts 2 and 3 and does not return until the middle of act 4. Edgar remains throughout much of the action of the central scenes, learning, as he must, what apparently Cordelia already knows about the ways of the world.

The significance as well as the organization of the dramatic structure, then, is the subject of chapter 3. The following chapter deals with thematic developments in *King Lear*. As extensive as this chapter is, it may not capture the themes' full range, for it is nearly impossible to discuss every aspect of this enormously rich and profound drama. Among the themes that are treated are: politics; bonds between family members, masters and servants, and others; social responsibility; the world of nature; and the contrasts between reason and madness. These are not by any means discrete thematic developments; they overlap and intertwine one with another in the tightly woven fabric of the play. But criticism requires that we treat them separately, at least at first, so that we may understand what it is we are discussing.

One theme not treated in chapter 4 is the theme of sight and insight, but this theme becomes the subject of linguistic analysis, one of several critical approaches described in chapter 5. Certainly an important subject, blindness—both literal and metaphorical—provides one of the issues that Robert Heilman treats in his analysis of the patterns of imagery in *This Great Stage*.[3] Similarly, the theme of incest, which some psychoanalytically oriented critics find in the play, is also treated in this chapter under the subheading Psychoanalytical Criticism. Gender and feminist criticism has made important contributions to our understanding of *King Lear*, particularly as it focuses on the issue of patriarchy. Besides imagery, other aspects of linguistic analysis are also significant, as critics such as Madeleine Doran and John Porter Houston show in their discussions of grammar and syntax.

The New Historicism has likewise made important contributions. Stephen Greenblatt's essay, *"King Lear* and the Exorcists," is one of the best of this kind, showing not only how Shakespeare adopted the language of Samuel Harsnett's *Declaration of Egregious Popish Impostures* (1603), but why he did. Cultural materialists like Terence Hawkes, somewhat allied to New Historicist approaches, have also found new avenues of approach to the play. One of the most fruitful approaches is that of myth and archetypal criticism. Unfortunately, no compilations of folktales and legends from Shakespeare's day are extant, for it is not until the nineteenth century that the subject began to interest scholars. This, of course, does not mean that Shakespeare and his contemporaries did not have access to the many stories and myths descending to them down the ages. The Lear story itself has been well documented as part of a whole congeries of legends sometimes grouped under the heading of "Love like Salt."[4] *King Lear* also has affinities with the Cinderella story, although that part of the legend may conclude as early as the end of the first scene.[5]

Critical approaches to the vexed problem of Christian references and allusions in *King Lear* have aroused a good deal of controversy. Some critics maintain that the play, though set in pre-Christian Britain, nevertheless was written and performed before a decidedly Christian audience, who would recognize the allusions and their significance. The issue centers on the character of Cordelia: Is she a Christ figure? Does she return to Britain to redeem her father from his sins and die doing so? Or does she represent the pagan *prisca theologica*, or "virtuous heathen" view, grounded in pre-Christian thought, which in some ways foreshadows Christian concepts of virtue, as William Elton maintains?[6] This chapter concludes by asking whether René Fortin provides a viable compromise, or reconciliation, of these opposed views.[7]

Finally, chapter 6 reviews in selective fashion *King Lear* in performance. Although it was once believed (and some still believe) that *King Lear* is too immense to be played on the professional stage, several recent productions tend to belie that argument. This chapter considers the various aspects of playing *King Lear* from Shakespeare's time to our own, noting in passing how the play has occasionally been rewritten to appeal more favorably to contemporary audiences. For example, finding the language and other matters in the play somewhat objectionable, including its harsh conclusion, Nahum Tate, in 1681, rewrote the tragedy to give it a happy ending. This ending held the stage for over a hundred years, both in Britain and America. The Fool was dropped; he was not reinstated, almost as an afterthought, until 1838 by William Charles Macready, and was played by Priscilla Horton. Since that time, Shakespeare's text has regained more and more ground, and occasionally either quarto or Folio texts have been performed rather than some version based upon a conflation of the two.[8]

King Lear has been filmed in notable productions by Peter Brook and the Russian director Grigori Kozintsev. The BBC-TV series reduced the play to some extent to accommodate the smaller television screen, as did the more recent production at the Royal National in the Cottesloe Theatre, presumably with the television adaptation in mind. Ian Holm played the lead and, despite his small size captured much of the grandeur and some of the titanism of Lear. Film, of course, has both advantages and disadvantages when compared with stage productions: the advantage of closeups and the technique of using voice-overs for soliloquies must be balanced against the audience's inability to view whatever it wants, as we can when watching a play on stage. Moreover, film productions tend to cut the text severely, replacing what is omitted with visuals of greater or lesser effectiveness.

Having taught Shakespeare for over forty years, and having edited *King Lear* three different times in three different ways, I have learned a lot about the play. But I am always amazed—and gratified—to discover that each time I am in a classroom and discuss the play with my students, or when I read the latest journal articles and books, how much more there is to learn. This book is an attempt to aid the reader in probing the depths of *King Lear*, not with any expectation that one will ever touch bottom—the play, like so many of Shakespeare's (with the exception of *A Midsummer Night's Dream*), is, after all, bottomless. But the effort of investigation is every bit worth the pains, and the hope here is that this book will help the reader become well enough oriented so that the search will become as fruitful as possible.

Because I have profited so much over the years from the many wonderful students I have had the great privilege of learning with—students at the Universities of Delaware, California (Davis), and Cyprus (where much of this book was written in the spring of 2000)—I gratefully dedicate this book to them—and to the members of the summer seminars for school teachers, sponsored by the National Endowment of the Humanities, with whom I studied the play during the last two decades.

George Butler kindly assigned this book to me and made useful suggestions after reading the typescript. David Palmer, my production editor, skillfully guided the book through the press. Margery Heffron was the copyeditor. To all of them, I here register my sincere gratitude.

NOTES

1. Harold Bloom, *Shakespeare: The Invention of the Human* (New York: Riverhead Books, 1998), p. 506.
2. Gary Taylor and Michael Warren, eds. *The Division of the Kingdoms* (Oxford: Clarendon Press, 1983).
3. Robert Bechtold Heilman, *This Great Stage: Image and Structure in "King Lear."* Seattle: University of Washington Press, 1963; rpt. Greenwood Press, 1976.

4. See, for example, Stith Thompson, *Motif-Index of Folk-Literature* (Bloomington: Indiana University Press, 1956), III, 432, and V, 29.

5. See Katherine Stockholder, "The Multiple Genres of *King Lear*: Breaking the Archetypes," *Bucknell Review* 16 (1968).

6. William R. Elton, *"King Lear" and the Gods* 2nd ed. (Lexington: University Press of Kentucky, 1988), pp. 38–42.

7. René Fortin, "Hermeneutical Circularity and Christian Interpretations of *King Lear*," in *Gaining upon Certainty: Selected Criticism* (Providence: Providence College Press, 1995), pp. 125–38.

8. In 1990, the Royal Shakespeare Company (RSC) tried to present a Folio-based production, but the actor playing Edgar insisted on retaining the speeches at the end of 3.6 that belong to that role. For a modern version of *King Lear* see Edward Bond's *Lear* (1971), which the RSC performed back-to-back with Shakespeare's *King Lear* in 1982 in Stratford-upon-Avon.

1

TEXTUAL HISTORY

THE TWO TEXTS OF "KING LEAR"

Shakespeare probably wrote *King Lear* sometime in 1605–06. Its first recorded performance is at court on St. Stephen's night (December 26) 1606, but it was probably staged at the Globe Theatre earlier. Under the date 26 November 1607, the play was entered in the Stationers' Register by Nathaniel Butter and John Busby, but the first printed version of the play appeared in 1608 from the press of Nicholas Okes. How he acquired the right to print *King Lear* is not known. His compositors—there were two of them—began printing the text in quarto in late 1607, were interrupted for a brief period to turn to another task, and resumed work in 1608 after the New Year.[1]

This first edition, referred to by scholars simply as Q1, or the "Pied Bull Quarto" (from the publisher's address on the title page), survives in a dozen copies, some with corrected pages, others with none. The title page reads:

M. William Shake-speare: / *HIS* / True Chronicle Historie of the life and / death of King LEAR and his three / Daughters. / *With the vnfortunate life of* Edgar, *sonne* / and heire to the Earle of Gloster, and his / sullen and assumed humor of / TOM of Bedlam / *As it was played before the Kings Maiestie at Whitethall vpon* / *S.* Stephans *night in Christmas Hollidayes.* / By his Maiesties seruants playing vsually at the Gloabe /on the Banck-side / [Printer's device] / *LONDON,* / Printed for *Nathaniel Butter,* and are to be sold at his

M. William Shak-speare:

HIS
True Chronicle Historie of the life and
death of King LEAR and his three
Daughters.

With the vnfortunate life of Edgar, *sonne*
and heire to the Earle of Gloster, and his
sullen and assumed humor of
TOM of Bedlam:

As it was played before the Kings Maiestie at Whitehall vpon
S. Stephans night in Christmas Hollidayes.

By his Maiesties seruants playing vsually at the Gloabe
on the Bancke-side.

LONDON,
Printed for *Nathaniel Butter*, and are to be sold at his shop in *Pauls*
Church-yard at the signe of the Pide Bull neere
St. *Austins* Gate. 1608.

Title page of the First Quarto (1608).

shop in *Pauls* / Church-yard at the signe of the Pide Bull neere / St. *Austins* Gate. 1 6 0 8.

Since Okes had never printed a playscript before, and since the copy he had was undoubtedly manuscript "foul papers," in other words, an authorial rough draft containing many lines overwritten with revisions, alterations, and corrections or substitutions crowded into margins, Okes's compositors had difficulty producing a clean and accurate edition. A good deal of verse is printed as prose and vice versa, and some words are obviously garbled or otherwise in error.

Q1 was followed many years later by a second quarto, Q2, in 1619 but falsely dated 1608. It was printed in William Jaggard's shop as part of an attempt by Jaggard's friend, Thomas Pavier, to collect Shakespeare's works. The project proved abortive and, foiled in his effort, Pavier tried to pass off the plays he had so far had printed by giving them the dates of earlier editions. Essentially a reprint of Q1, the so-called Pavier quarto of *King Lear* (Q2) has no textual authority, even though it corrects some of Q1's most obvious errors and, in the Dover Beach scene, includes a unique two-word speech: "*Gent.* Good Sir." inserted after Lear's quarto-only line "Ay, and laying autumn's dust" (4.5.188a). The speech may reflect a corrected state of Q1 that has not survived.[2]

Another and quite different version of *King Lear* appeared in the great Folio of 1623, an authoritative collection of Shakespeare's works by his fellow shareholders in the King's Men, John Heminge and Henry Condell. The differences between Q1 and F (as the Folio is referred to) are considerable, so that for a long time many scholars believed that each version was an incomplete or corrupt text of some lost original. More recent scholarship rejects this theory in favor of a two-text theory.[3] That is, Shakespeare revised the text of Q1, cutting some lines, adding others, and often altering words or phrases throughout. Most likely the play was revised more than once, possibly by others as well as its original author, over a period of years as it was revived for performance in different venues or for different occasions. This is, after all, typical of theatrical practice, then as now.

DIFFERENCES BETWEEN QUARTO AND FOLIO *KING LEAR*

F cuts about 300 lines from Q1 and adds another 100, so that it is about 200 lines shorter. While shortening may have motivated some of the cuts, especially in the latter half of the play, the play in F is still very long, much longer than the usual Elizabethan or Jacobean drama. Only Ben Jonson's plays rival Shakespeare's in surpassing the typical length of plays staged in the period. Other motives must therefore have occasioned the revisions, including both deletions and additions, as well as local alterations. For example, many of the alterations in the Folio text reveal significant changes in the characterization of principal leads. Perhaps most noteworthy are the changes in the characters of Albany and Edgar. Whereas in Q1 Albany's lines in 4.2 show him far more forceful, for example, in the way he dresses down his wife Gonerill, his speeches are much curtailed in F. Elsewhere, too, omissions in F weaken his character, making him appear less able or strong. By contrast, Edgar's character as it emerges in F is strengthened, so that by the very end of the play, he appears to have earned the right to deliver the concluding four lines, which in Q1 are given to Albany.[4]

Gonerill's character also differs between the two versions. In Q1 her disposition is even nastier than it appears in F where, for example, some effort is made to justify her actions against King Lear, as at the end of 1.4, when she dismisses her husband's concern that she is overreacting to her father's behavior. She is still a wicked daughter; no question about that. But Shakespeare seems to allow her a greater degree of rationalization—and it is only that—for what she does in F.[5]

The Fool's part has perhaps more noticeable changes, and these include additions as well as cuts. In 1.4 his satire against monopolies and court immorality disappears from F, possibly because King James and his courtiers may have found it too offensive. (Censorship is an issue that will bear further discussion below.) On the other hand, Merlin's prophecy at the end of 3.2 seems an odd interpolation at a point shortly before other speeches, such as Edgar's moralizing in 3.6, are omitted. Some scholars have defended it as a summary view of the topsy-turvy world of *King Lear*, thematically justified,[6] while others regard it as an interpolation, possibly not by Shakespeare. Whatever the case, the Fool's last line, "And I'll go to bed at noon" (3.6.41), added in F, provides him with an excellent closing line. Since the Fool never appears again in the play in either text, Shakespeare may have decided, during the process of revision, to give him the line. Or perhaps the Folio compositor skipped the line while setting type.

The title role, King Lear, also reveals significant changes between Q1 and F. As Thomas Clayton says, "In no case are the additions or revisions in Lear's part without dramatic purpose, theatrical effect, and thematic significance, and even the numerous 'minor' changes in wording are almost never 'indifferent variants.' "[7] His analysis of Lear's first long speech in 1.1 shows a "complex of effects": the changes in F, including its significant additional lines, anticipate the king's firmness demonstrated later on in the play, both his "hideous rashness" (1.1.145) as well as his determination to be "the pattern of all patience" (3.2.35). The Folio version of 1.1.31–49 also lays the foundation for the development of sympathy for Lear who, however mistaken, explains his motive for dividing up his kingdom as an attempt to prevent "future strife" among his daughters, who will inherit the land. But even more significant are the changes at the end of the play in the reordering of speeches and the additional lines F gives Lear. Here is the way Q1 prints the speeches:[8]

> *Lear.* And my poore foole is hangd, no, no life, why should a dog, a horse, a rat of life and thou no breath at all, O thou wilt come no more, neuer, neuer, neuer, pray you vndo this button, thanke you sir, O,o,o,o. *Edg.* He faints my Lord, my Lord.
>
> *Lear.* Breake hart, I prethe breake. *Edgar.* Look vp my Lord.

This is the Folio revision:

> *Lear.* And my poore Foole is hang'd: no, no, no life?
> Why should a Dog, a Horse, a Rat haue life,
> And thou no breath at all? Thou'lt come no more,
> Neuer, neuer, neuer, neuer, neuer.
> Pray you vndo this Button. Thank you Sir,
> Do you see this? Looke on her? Looke her lips,
> Looke there, looke there.   *He dies.*
>
> *Edg.* He faints, my Lord, my Lord.
>
> *Kent.* Breake heart, I prythee breake.
>
> *Edg.* Looke vp my Lord.

Although Q's rendition of the ending is intelligible and satisfactory in itself, as Clayton notes (p. 129), F's reading is superior in many ways. It brings the movement of the play full circle. Whereas in the opening scene Lear directed attention to himself, asking his daughters to proclaim how much they love him, at the end he directs attention to his beloved Cordelia: "Looke there, looke there," he says, and dies.

During the reigns of Elizabeth I and James I all plays were subject to licensing by the Master of the Revels, who could, if he found anything objectionable in them, refuse to allow them to be performed until suitably revised. Did *King Lear* undergo such treatment? Or did the King's Men exercise self-censorship? They surely understood the rules of the game; after all, the king himself was their patron. The issue becomes acute when we consider the alterations involving references to France invading England. James I regarded himself as the peacemaker of Europe, and, under his rule, England tried very hard to bring about some sort of rapprochement with France. Traditional enemies for centuries—one has only to think of the Shakespeare's earlier English history plays, such as *King Henry V*, to recall the enmity between the two countries—England and France after James's accession were, for a while, no longer at war with each other. When the play was performed at court, possibly references to their ancient enmity would be found disturbing, if not intolerable. Q1 includes a number of such references that F omits, suggesting that among the earliest revisions were those that toned down France's invasion of England. True, as E.A.J. Honigmann has said, when the forces under Cordelia appear in act 4, their banners would doubtless have shown it was the forces of France that had landed at Dover, but otherwise explicit references to that country all but disappear in F.[9] On the other hand, Gary Taylor argues that F's omission of Edmond's "Fut" in 1.2 is probably a direct result of official censorship, but the only one.[10]

THE TRANSMISSION OF THE TEXTS

The transmission of the texts to modern editions is a rather complicated affair, punctuated with supposition and conjecture, as often is the case in dealing with Shakespeare's plays and those of his contemporaries. Lacking Shakespeare's manuscripts, scholars have only the printed versions of the plays to go by. They may infer from various aspects of these editions what kinds of copy the printer had, how closely it was followed, what liberties were taken by compositors who often had to guess at words and their meanings, and so forth. We are reasonably certain that the Q1 copy was Shakespeare's own manuscript, which Okes's printers did the best they could with—and their best was none too good. From that point on, the trail becomes even more interesting. Meanwhile, a fair copy of the play was made, either by Shakespeare or a theatrical scribe, and this copy became the promptbook that was evidently used in the theater, modified most likely from time to time in rehearsals.

From various kinds of evidence we can assume that Shakespeare used one of the printed quartos of 1608 on which to make further revisions at a later period, possibly as early as 1609–10, when the King's Men began using their new, alternative venue in Blackfriars. This was a smaller, more "private" theater than the Globe, enclosed where the other was large and open to the sky. Some of the cuts, like those at the end of acts three and four, suggest the use of intervals between the acts, a feature of performances at Blackfriars and only later at the Globe. Shakespeare began tinkering with the play, as writers will do when revising, making many small, often trivial alterations as well as larger, significant changes.[11] Among some of the major cuts are the omission of all of 4.3 in Q1, where Kent and the Gentleman discuss Cordelia's return to England and her reaction to the condition of her father. Additions include the Fool's prophecy at the end of 3.2 and Lear's last lines, providing the switch from Kent to Lear of an important speech at that moment. Some of the language was made simpler, such as the change from *dearne* to *stern* 3.7.62. In one instance, a number of lines in F seem to have been substituted for others in Q1. This occurs in 3.1, where Kent is speaking to the Gentleman, but the anomaly may be the result of the Folio compositor failing to recognize how that speech was revised and erroneously making a substitution instead of including all the lines as intended.[12]

The revised copy of Q1 then presumably became the basis for a new promptbook. Either it, or more likely a transcription of it, became the copy for F, which was set up in type by two compositors using cast off copy.[13] One of the compositors has been identified (through the use of spelling preferences and other data) as Compositor B in Jaggard's printing shop, which produced the Folio. He was not the most careful compositor and sometimes took liberties with his copy, occasionally cramming more lines into the space available on his page, or contriwise, spreading his copy to fill up an oversupply of space. The other compositor Charlton K. Hinman has identified as Compositor E, an apprentice, who had difficulty following manuscript copy.[14] Since Jaggard's print shop was also responsible for producing the Pavier quartos, a copy of Q2 was evidently available for consultation by Jaggard's Folio compositors, who followed its spelling and other aspects of printing when they needed to do so. A diagram, or stemma, of the transmission of the texts, somewhat simplified, appears below. The dotted lines indicate probable influence rather than direct descent.[15]

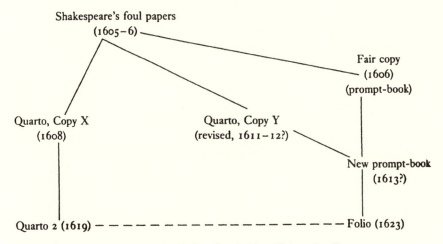

Shakespeare's foul papers
(1605–6)

Fair copy
(1606)
(prompt-book)

Quarto, Copy X   Quarto, Copy Y
(1608)   (revised, 1611–12?)

New prompt-book
(1613?)

Quarto 2 (1619) – Folio (1623)

From *KING LEAR*, ed. Jay L. Halio, Cambridge University Press.

    The Folio of 1623 was an important and expensive book. It took nine years for all of its copies to be sold off before a second edition was printed (F2) in 1632. Like Q2, F2 and subsequent reprintings in 1663–64 (F3) and 1685 (F4) have no textual authority. They correct some obvious errors and introduce others. Where the corrections are self-evident, modern editors adopt them, recording their origin in a note or in collations beneath the text or immediately following it.

    Modern editing of the plays began with Nicholas Rowe's edition of 1709, followed a few years later by his own revised editions and then by the editions of Alexander Pope, Lewis Theobald, Thomas Hanmer, William Warburton, Edward Capell, Samuel Johnson, George Steevens, and Edmond Malone in the eighteenth century. The earliest editors, most notoriously Pope, often "improved" Shakespeare's text, following the decorum of their own time, and corrected versification they believed needed regularizing. Being highly suspicious of actors' interpolations as well as printers' carelessness, these editors justified their emendations, as often as not writing detailed explanations to defend them.

    Modern editors since the eighteenth century have been reluctant to omit anything that Shakespeare undoubtedly wrote; their attitude derives mainly from the one-text theory of a lost original for which Q1 and F provide incomplete versions. Therefore, most editions of *King Lear* since Pope's generally conflate, or combine, both Q1 and F. These conflated editions, which appear in many standard textbooks today, such as the

Riverside, Bevington, and Pelican editions, present a version of the play that Shakespeare never saw or expected to see staged.[16] They overlook the fact that anomalies are present in such conflations, such as the splicing of Q1 and F versions of Kent's long speech in 3.1.[17] Editors usually also offer an electic text, taking readings from either Q1 or F that seem to them preferable on literary grounds, rather than scrupulously following either Q1 or F. Of course, any edition that attempts to follow just one version must on occasion borrow from the other authoritative version when the control text—the one the editor has chosen to follow—is obviously in error.[18] Hence, an editor like Russell Fraser, whose conflated Signet edition relies chiefly on the F text, adopts corrected Q's "clamorous" at 2.2.20 instead of F's "clamours," which is obviously wrong. Occasionally, neither Q1 nor F has got the wording right and editors must resort to emendation. For example, neither "miseries" (F) nor "mistress" (Q) is correct at 1.1.104, and "mysteries" (F2) is the correct reading, which all modern editors accept and emend their texts accordingly.

Among recent single-play editions of *King Lear* currently available are the New Arden, edited by R. A. Foakes; the New Oxford, edited by Stanley Wells and Gary Taylor; René Weiss's parallel-text edition; and my New Cambridge Shakespeare. Foakes's edition (Arden 3) offers a conflated text, but with Q and F lines clearly designated by superscript letters. Wells and Taylor's volume is a Q-based text, and my New Cambridge is F-based. All of these editions are fully annotated. My Q-based edition, *The First Quarto of King Lear* (Cambridge University Press, 1994), has textual notes only, but Weiss's parallel-text edition has some other annotations as well. The new Folger Shakespeare (1993), edited by Barbara Mowat and Paul Werstine, has a conflated text with Q and F passages indicated and with annotations on the facing page, a format that John F. Andrews also adopts for his Everyman edition (1993). The Signet, Pelican, and other older single-play editions all have conflated texts.

NOTES

1. See Peter W. M. Blayney, *The Texts of "King Lear" and Their Origins*, 2 vols. (Cambridge: Cambridge University Press, 1982), I, 148–49.

2. On the interesting problem of the variant pages in Q1 *Lear*, that is, the copies which contain corrected and/or uncorrected sheets from Okes's printing press, see W. W. Greg, *The Variants in the First Quarto of "King Lear"* (Oxford: Clarendon Press, 1940).

3. For discussions of the two-text theory as against the older theory of a single lost original, see the essays in *The Division of the Kingdoms: Shakespeare's Two Versions of "King Lear,"* ed. Gary Taylor and Michael Warren (Oxford: Clarendon Press, 1983); Stephen Urkowitz, *Shakespeare's Revision of "King Lear"* (Princeton: Princeton University Press, 1980); and Grace Ioppolo, *Revising Shakespeare*, (Cambridge, Mass.: Harvard University Press, 1991).

4. See Michael Warren, "Quarto and Folio *King Lear* and the Interpretation of Albany and Edgar," in *Shakespeare: Pattern of Excelling Nature*, ed. David Bevington and Jay L. Halio (Newark: University of Delaware Press, 1978), pp. 95–107.

5. See Randall McLeod, " 'No more, the text is foolish,' " in Taylor and Warren, *Division*, pp. 153–93.

6. For example, Joseph Wittreich, *"Image of That Horror": History, Prophecy, and Apocalypse in "King Lear"* (San Marino, Calif.: Huntington Library, 1984), pp. 47–74. See also John Kerrigan, "Revision, Adaptation, and the Fool in *King Lear*," in Taylor and Warren, *Division*, pp. 195–239.

7. Thomas Clayton, " 'Is this the promis'd end?' Revision in the Role of the King," in Warren and Taylor, *Division*, p. 122. See also Alexander Leggatt, "Two Lears: Notes for an Actor," in *Shakespeare: Text and Performance*, ed. Lois Potter and Arthur F. Kinney (Newark: University of Delaware Press, 1999), pp. 310–19, for another detailed analysis of this and Lear's other speeches as they differ between Q and F.

8. I have preserved the original spellings in both Q and F. Note that Q prints the lines as prose, whereas F correctly prints them as verse. Q crowds Edgar's short speeches into the available space after Lear's lines. See Clayton, p. 128, or the facsimile of these lines in my edition, p. 75.

9. See Honigman's review of *The Division of the Kingdoms*, "Do-it-yourself-*Lear*" in *The New York Review of Books*, 25 October 1990, p. 59.

10. Taylor, "The war in *King Lear*," *Shakespeare Survey* 33 (1980), 27–34, and "Monopolies, Show Trials, Disaster, and Invasion: *King Lear* and Censorship," in Taylor and Warren, *Division*, pp. 75–119, especially pp. 109–10.

11. See Kerrigan, "Revision," pp. 205–17.

12. See Richard Knowles, "Revision Gone Awry in Folio *Lear* 3.1," *Shakespeare Quarterly* 46 (1995), 32–46. In this essay, acknowledging his debt to Peter Blayney's suggestions, Knowles shows how the lines unique to Q1 and F may be properly arranged as a single, revised speech. Although Knowles generally accepts the revision theory, he does not believe that Shakespeare was the reviser or that all the changes were made at the same time or by one and the same person. Knowles is the editor of the forthcoming New Variorum edition of *King Lear*.

13. Casting off copy was a process whereby estimates were made of how much text would fit on a page, and then appropriate portions were distributed among the compositors for setting. Since the Folio pages were not set seriatim,

this procedure had to be followed. For explanation of how the Folio was printed using cast off copy, see Charlton Hinman's introduction to *The Norton Facsimile: The First Folio of Shakespeare* (New York: W. W. Norton, 1968), p. xvi.

14. Hinman, "The Prentice Hand in the Tragedies of the Shakespeare First Folio:Compositor E," *Studies in Bibliography* 9 (1957), 3–20; but see also Hinman's later work on the compositors for *King Lear* in *The Printing and Proofreading of the First Folio of Shakespeare*, 2 vols. (Oxford: Oxford University Press, 1963), pp. 200–06.

15. The diagram is from my New Cambridge edition of *King Lear*, p. 70. On the use of Q2 in the printing of F, see Gary Taylor, "Folio Compositors and Folio Copy: *King Lear* and its Context," *Publications of the Bibliographical Society of America* 79 (1985), 17–74, and the discussion in my edition, pp. 63–68, which cites other scholars on the subject.

16. Notable exceptions are *William Shakespeare: The Complete Works*, ed. Stanley Wells, Gary Taylor et al. (Oxford: Oxford University Press, 1986), which prints both a Q-based and an F-based text of *King Lear*, and my New Cambridge Shakespeare edition (1992), which is based upon F and prints Q-only passages in an Appendix. The Norton *Complete Works*, ed. Stephen Greenblatt et al. (New York, 1997), adopts the Oxford texts, but also prints a third, conflated text.

17. See analysis of these passages in my New Cambridge edition, pp. 269–70, and compare Richard Knowles's ingenious defense of their conflation (note 12, above).

18. See Jay L. Halio, "Shakespeare's Elusive Text: A Response to [David] Bevington's Critique of the new Oxford Complete Works," *Shakespeare Bulletin* 6 (May/June 1988), 5–6.

2

CONTEXTS AND SOURCES

THE PLACE OF *KING LEAR* IN THE SHAKESPEARE CANON

Although scholars cannot precisely date the composition of Shake-speare's plays and, therefore, we cannot be absolutely certain of their chronology, both internal and external indicators help us to form what is generally accepted as the probable order of their genesis. *Titus Andronicus*, for example, is one of the earliest plays in the canon, usually dated about 1590–92. It is Shakespeare's first tragedy. A tragedy of blood revenge, *Titus Andronicus* antedates *Hamlet* by almost a decade and more closely resembles in theme and structure Thomas Kyd's famous revenge play, *The Spanish Tragedy* (*ca.* 1588). Several years later, Shakespeare essayed another tragedy, *Romeo and Juliet*, which is one of three plays of his so-called lyrical group. While it also concerns itself heavily with the theme of revenge, it is entirely different from *Titus Andronicus* and from many of the tragedies that followed later at the turn of the century and afterwards. Classified as a history play and grouped with the second *Henriad*—plays that also include *Henry IV*, Parts I and II, and *Henry V*—*Richard II* may also be considered a tragedy, but again it is unlike the later plays in that genre and more closely resembles Christopher Marlowe's *Edward II* (1592–93).

Shakespeare turned more directly and thoroughly to the composition of tragedy with *Julius Caesar* (1599) while he was also completing his group of "joyous" comedies—*Much Ado about Nothing* (1598), *As You Like It* (1599), and *Twelfth Night* (1600). Thereafter, although he continued to write some comedies, such as *All's Well That Ends Well* (1602) and *Measure for Measure* (1603), these are unlike his earlier plays in that genre. They are much darker in subject matter and treatment and involve moral issues so inadequately resolved that they are often referred to as "problem plays," like those of the modern dramatist Henrik Ibsen. It is during this period that Shakespeare seems to have become far more interested in writing tragedies, though no satisfactory reason has yet been offered to explain this shift in the direction of his work. If critics once believed that Shakespeare had entered a period of deep personal crisis, that theory is no longer credited. He was now at the peak of his powers and highly successful, having bought expensive property in Stratford and persuaded the College of Heralds to allow him a coat of arms and the title of "Gentleman."[1] His son Hamnet's death in 1596 would have been more likely to plunge the dramatist into depression, for, as his plays repeatedly show, he was much concerned with the continuation of the family line. But at the time of his only son's early death and immediately afterwards, Shakespeare was writing his happiest comedies and history plays.

King Lear, dated approximately 1605–06, falls midway between *Othello* and *Macbeth* among the great tragedies. In many respects, it represents a transitional drama between the middle tragedies—*Julius Caesar, Hamlet*, and *Othello*—and the later tragedies, or what Willard Farnham has called the plays of "Shakespeare's tragic frontier"—*Macbeth, Timon of Athens, Antony and Cleopatra*, and *Coriolanus*.[2] One of the salient characteristics of the middle tragedies, those preceding *King Lear*, is that the tragic protagonist does not see, or sees only obliquely, an alternative action that might prevent disaster. Brutus in *Julius Caesar* never recognizes any other alternative to the assassination plot against Caesar. Although later on, in his conflict with Cassius in act 4, he confronts his friend and coconspirator directly concerning a dispute between them, it does not occur to Brutus that this might be an avenue of approach to Caesar instead of killing him outright. In *Hamlet*, after killing Polonius, the Prince obliquely recognizes that he must be both "scourge and minister" to Denmark.[3] But by then, it is too late. Had he acted against Claudius in the prayer scene as he has just done with his mother, Gertrude, in the closet scene, perhaps tragedy could have been averted.[4] Earlier, when Rosencrantz and Guildenstern approach him after "The Murder of Gonzago," the play within the play, he jokes about being Claudius's physician (3.4.290–94), failing to see this as his proper role in ministering to the morally infected king and helping to cure the disease that is starting to spread throughout Denmark.

Othello's behavior resembles that of his immediate forebears in Shakespearean tragedy. If Ned B. Allen is correct,[5] and Shakespeare wrote acts 1 and 2 *after* acts 3–5, then the first two acts serve as a commentary on the last three. In act 1, Othello is confident of his position. Facing Brabantio's charges before the Duke of Venice and his court, he calmly says, "Send for the lady"—his wife, Desdemona—to let her testify directly concerning those charges. When Desdemona arrives, she confirms everything that Othello has said in the interim, and the issue is resolved. In act 2, after the brawl has been quieted and Othello is fully in charge, he demands to know what has caused it. He holds a kind of summary court martial and, given an account of events that no one present contradicts, including the principals in the quarrel, he assumes—wrongly, but understandably—that Cassio is entirely at fault. He thereupon precipitously cashiers him. This action gives Iago the opportunity he wants and has planned for, and he proceeds accordingly in the next three acts. When, convinced that Desdemona has committed adultery with Cassio, Othello enters their bedchamber to murder his wife, Desdemona cries out, "Send for the man" (5.2.52), echoing Othello's words in act 1. This failure to do so, to follow the procedure he has himself done earlier, leads directly to the catastrophe.

In *King Lear*, action moves swiftly in the opening scene, as Lear loses no time in expelling Cordelia from his presence. Blind with rage, he refuses to listen to her carefully argued logic: "Why have my sisters husbands, if they say / They love you all?" (1.1.94–5). When Kent intervenes, clearly pointing out Lear's folly, and shouting "See better, Lear, and let me still remain / The true blank of thine eye" (1.1.151–2), he is also banished for his pains. The alternatives to disaster that Kent plainly indicates—"Reserve thy state, / And in thy best consideration check / This hideous rashness" (1.1.143–5)—Lear utterly rejects. Enraged, headstrong, embarrassed before his assembled court, Lear refuses to follow Kent's admonition to "see better" and plunges right on. His blindness is a result of wilfulness, of a failure to heed the alternatives to disaster that he might have chosen, were he other than the man he is, and that have been open and obvious to everyone else. Lear thus represents a new kind of protagonist in the development of Shakespeare's tragedies, unlike those who have preceded him insofar as he has the alternatives to disaster delineated directly before him, only to reject them.

Following the composition of *King Lear*, Shakespeare continues to experiment in *Macbeth* with this new kind of tragic hero. Macbeth is fully aware from the outset what his alternatives are. But, unlike Lear, he needs no one to tell him what they are. He knows what a "deep damnation" killing Duncan—his king, his kinsman, and his guest— means (1.7.12–20). Although he hesitates at first, his wife urges him on, and under her determined will, he follows through. Later on, he recognizes that it is not too late to turn back, but he finds it too "tedious" (3.4.139), worn out as he is with sleeplessness and fatigue. And so he plunges on to more and more reckless murder, leading ultimately his own death. Similarly, Antony in *Antony and Cleopatra* knows what he, as one of the triple pillars of the world, should do rather than remain in Egypt, "the bellows and the fan / To cool a gypsy's lust," as one of his men laments (1.1.9–10). For a while, he does shake off those Egyptian fetters and returns to confront Octavius Caesar and reclaim his proper position, marrying Caesar's sister to confirm his renewed status. But the arrangement does not last long. Like Lear, he later fails to listen to the good advice of his soldiers when facing the threat of Octavius's armed forces, and his wilfulness ends in his suicide and then Cleopatra's.

Scholars are less certain about where the composition of *Timon of Athens* fits in Shakespeare's chronology. It is apparently an unfinished piece of work and may never have been staged. It bears similarities to *King Lear* not only in the deep pessimism that Timon expresses in the second half of the play, which associates him with the earl of Gloucester; it also presents a protagonist who refuses to heed the strong arguments of his steward to relent and stop giving away his fortune, actions that lead to his ruin and the abdication of his presumed friends. *Coriolanus* shows a further development in the tragic protagonist. Unlike Lear and Timon, he seems willing, however reluctantly, to heed the advice of his mother and others, who want him to stand for consul of the Roman republic. But he finds it impossible to violate his true nature, to humble himself before the tribunes and the plebians to the extent that is required to win the election and, under provocation, he lashes out against them. This leads to his banishment and his defection to his former enemy, Aufidius, leader of the Corioles, who then use him in their continuing battle against Rome. But, again, unlike his predecessors in Shakespearean tragedy, at the crucial moment of decision, when he stands before his mother and the rest of his family, who plead on behalf of mercy for Rome, Coriolanus relents. He sees an alternative to common disaster, he believes, and makes the right decision, not to destroy Rome but to make peace. While this decision leads to his death, it is the only death that occurs in this tragedy and provides a link to the late romances, or tragicomedies, that follow in the canon[6]—*Cymbeline* (1609), *The Winter's Tale* (1610), and *The Tempest* (1611). These three plays conclude Shakespeare's dramatic career, except for *Henry VIII* (1612–13) and *The Two Noble Kinsmen* (1613) that he apparently came out of retirement to write in collaboration with his fellow dramatist, John Fletcher.

THE HISTORICAL CONTEXT

When James VI of Scotland came to the English throne after Elizabeth I's death in 1603 as James I of England, he was determined to unite the two kingdoms over which he now ruled. But his experiences as King of Scotland had badly prepared him to govern England. Even during Elizabeth I's reign, Parliament had begun the struggle for power that culminated in the next century in the execution of Charles I and the English civil war. Fashioning himself as an absolute monarch by divine right, James came into direct conflict with his English subjects, who rejected this view of himself as "above the law, above the church, above the Parliament."[7] Moreover, for centuries, England and Scotland had been bitter enemies, and skirmishes along their common border were the rule, when open warfare did not utterly engage the two kingdoms.

As a result of James's wishes, the Parliament of 1606–1607 spent much of its time on the question of uniting the two realms, Scotland and England. James proposed four preliminary steps toward effecting that union: repeal of hostile laws that had been promulgated by both kingdoms, mutual naturalization of their subjects, a treaty promoting free trade between the kingdoms, and improvement of the administration of justice on both sides of the border.[8] He was successful in realizing only the first of these goals. He never came close to fulfilling the ultimate aim of complete union. D. H. Willson succinctly sums up what James wanted and what he did not get:

> James would have one kingdom with one king, one faith, one language, one people alike in manners and allegiance. The names of England and Scotland should disappear in the name of Britain. . . . But James was in too much of a hurry. He forgot the long and mutual hostility of the two nations.[9]

Because of this longstanding enmity, James's English subjects were less than eager to form the union their king so earnestly desired. In addition, James antagonized his English subjects by bringing with him a large number of Scots whom he treated with excessive generosity, much to the disgust and envy of the English courtiers. He was therefore unable, but not for lack of trying, to get Parliament to agree to unification and pass a bill to that effect. It was not until the eighteenth century, in fact, that this union was established (1707).

The performance of *King Lear* at court on St. Stephens's Day during the Christmas holidays of 1606 would thus have struck James and his courtiers powerfully, from the very first moments, during which the earls of Gloucester and Kent discuss the division of the kingdom, on to the very end of the play. The king would have recognized at once Lear's folly and sympathized completely with Kent when he tries to intervene and get Lear to "reverse his doom," that is, to change his decision, not only to banish his best-loved daughter, Cordelia, but to divide up his kingdom among his two other daughters. By the beginning of act 2, as we learn from the discussion between Edmond and Curran, trouble is already brewing between the dukes of Albany and Cornwall, rivals for supreme power in the land. Lear's "fast intent" to divide his kingdom and thereby prevent "future strife" (1.1.33–40) is shown to be what it is: a fool's dream, however well intentioned.

Other aspects of the play would have struck home as well. In October 1603, Sir Brian Annesley's daughter, Lady Grace Wildgoose (or Wildgose), tried to have her father certified as incompetent and committed to the care of herself and her husband. Opposing this action was Sir Brian's youngest daughter, Cordell. An old retainer of Queen Elizabeth I, Annesley held valuable property in Kent, ostensibly the object of his eldest daughter's desire to have him committed. He had a second daughter, Christian, but what part she played in this affair is not known. Nevertheless, the story of an old man and his three daughters directly parallels the story of King Lear. Sir Brian died in 1604, leaving everything to his youngest daughter; whereupon, Lady Wildgoose contested the will, which was eventually upheld. One of the executors of the will, interestingly, was Sir William Harvey, who was married to the Countess of Pembroke, mother of Shakespeare's patron, the earl of Pembroke. When the countess died a few years later in 1607, Sir William married Cordell Annesley.

It is unlikely that the Annesley case was unique. In *King Lear* 1.2.65–7, Edmond tells his father that he has heard Edgar speak about the way "sons at perfect age, and fathers declined, the father should be as ward to the son, and the son manage his revenue." Gloucester believes Edmond, and the episode suggests that this was a topic of some interest at the time Shakespeare wrote the play, as it has been down through the ages into the present. The close similarity of the names Cordell and Cordelia, reminding him of the Lear story, may have suggested the parallel to Shakespeare, although the incident must have been notorious at the time he began thinking about a play on King Lear.

Other contemporary events also influenced the composition of this play. In 1603 Samuel Harsnett published *A Declaration of Egregious Popish Impostures*. It is a tract vigorously exposing what Harsnett tried to prove were fraudulent exorcisms practiced by Catholic priests in England going back as far as 1585–86. His principal targets were the prosletyzing Catholics who used the "miracle" of exorcism to convert Anglicans to the Church of Rome. Harsnett set out to prove that what passed for successful exorcisms were nothing more than theatrical performances staged for the benefit of the innocent and unsophisticated audiences who observed them. The language of the supposed victims of possession by devils, which Harsnett quotes in his *Declaration*, is echoed repeatedly in the language that Edgar uses in act 3 when he assumes the role of Tom o'Bedlam.[10] Coincidentally (or not), one of the priests that Harsnett attacks in his book was Father William Weston, alias Edmunds, who performed his exorcisms in the household of Sir Edward Peckham. Edgar's mad speech, of course, is a performance, just as Harsnett claimed that the alleged victims that Father Edmunds had exorcised were also acting in an assumed role.

SOURCES AND ANALOGUES

The immediate source for the main plot of *King Lear* is *The True Chronicle History of King Leir*, an old play that was performed in the early 1590s but not published until 1605. But the Lear story has many much earlier antecedents, going back as far as Geoffrey of Monmouth's *Historia Regum Brittaniae* (History of Great Britain, c. 1135). As no English translation was available to Shakespeare, he may have read Geoffrey's account of the ancient King Leir in the original Latin or got details of the story from more recent writers who borrowed from the *Historia*.[11] Geoffrey was primarily interested not in the dysfunctional family as much as in the political situation that developed from Leir's division of the kingdom, which led directly to conflict between the two dukes, husbands of his elder daughters. He does not omit the love contest, which finds Cordeilla wooed and won by the King of France, where Leir joins her after the elder two daughters begin to strip him of his rights and dignities. Cordeilla welcomes her father, forgiving him his rash action in banishing her, and proceeds to win back for him his throne. When he dies three years later, Cordeilla succeeds him.

This happy outcome, followed in all subsequent accounts before Shakespeare, does not end there. The sons of Cordeilla's sisters, Margan and Cunedag, foment a rebellion and throw their aunt into prison, where in despair she commits suicide. The two cousins renew the conflict that their fathers began, and internecine strife resumes. Not until Margan is killed does peace come to Britain at last. But by that time, much of the land has been ruined and many lives lost. One can gather from this brief account of events how the political situation must have struck Shakespeare, whose version of a land divided would certainly have appealed to his company's patron, James I, who was trying so hard at that time to prevent the kind of problems that come from a divided kingdom.

The story of Leir and his three daughters became popular enough over the centuries to be repeated in various forms by numerous authors. It appears, along with Cordeilla's suicide, in Raphael Holinshed's *Chronicles of England, Scotland, and Wales*, which Shakespeare mined (he used the second edition of 1587 for many of his plays, such as *Macbeth*, and for his ten English history plays). In Holinshed's account, King Leir (the spelling authors usually used before Shakespeare) holds the love contest, in which Gonorilla and Regan insincerely swear their great love for their father, but Cordeilla replies in honesty and truth; whereupon Leir marries his elder daughters to the dukes of Cornwall and Albany, giving them his kingdom to divide as their inheritance when he should die. He leaves Cordeilla, whom he loved most, nothing; but the king of Gallia (France), hearing of her "beauty, womanhood, and good conditions," marries her despite the absence of any dowry. After some time, impatient to inherit the kingdom, his sons-in-law revolt against Leir and depose him, dividing the kingdom between them. Upset at his elder daughters' acquiescence in the plan to have their father live under humiliating conditions, to the extent that "they would scarcely allow one servant to wait upon him," Leir flees to France, where Cordeilla forgives and receives him. Her husband prepares a strong military force to be used against the dukes, who die in the battle, and Leir is restored to his throne, which Cordeilla inherits instead of her sisters after Leir's death.

The Leir story also appears in Higgins's *Mirror for Magistrates*, Spenser's *The Faerie Queene* (II.10.27–33), and other works. In all of these accounts, King Leir does not die before he regains his throne, and it is his youngest daughter, not the others, who wins the war. Why Shakespeare altered this ending, influenced perhaps by the subsequent death of Cordeilla in his source, we shall have to consider in a later chapter.

The Chronicle History of King Leir, the old play that likewise borrowed from these sources, generally follows the outline of events while it elaborates on many of them. Unlike Shakespeare's, this older anonymous play is heavily pietistic and ends with Leir and his companions going off to meditate together, leaving Cordella (as her name is spelled there) to reign in his stead. Her sisters and their husbands do not die, but after Cordella's victory they become fugitives and disappear from the action. Other divergences between Shakespeare's play and this are worth noting, such as several melodramatic events, for example Gonorill and Ragan's plot to murder their father (only briefly suggested in Shakespeare's play). No Fool appears in the old play, but Shakespeare may have got the idea for this character from Mumford, the jesting companion to the King of Gaul (France). The Gallian King has a much more substantial role in the old play than Shakespeare's King of France, who appears only 1.1. His ambassador, who invites Leir to join his daughter in France, and whose wanderings in Cornwall and Cambria may have suggested the nighttime journeys in Shakespeare's second act, does not appear at all in *King Lear*. In another difference between the two plays, Kent's counterpart, Perillus, is not banished but remains in his proper person with Leir and at the end is recognized for his service and rewarded.

For some of the flavor of *King Lear* as well as an instance of its melodramatic qualities, consider the following excerpt from Scene 24 (spelling and punctuation are modernized). Leir and Perillus, who have fled the enmity of the elder daughters, find themselves in France, alone and starving:

> *Leir.* Ah, my Perillus, now I see we both
> Shall end our days in this unfruitful soil.
> Oh, I do faint for want of sustenance:
> And thou, I know, in little better case.
> No gentle tree affords one taste of fruit
> To comfort us until we meet with men;
> No lucky path conducts our luckless steps
> Unto a place where any comfort dwells.

Sweet rest betide unto our happy souls,
For here I see our bodies must have end.

Perillus. Ah, my dear lord, how doth my heart lament
To see you brought to this extremity.
O, if you do love me, as you do profess,
Or ever thought well of me in my life,
Feed on this flesh, whose veins are not so dry
But there is virtue left to comfort you.
O feed on this [*offering his arm*], if this will do you good,
I'll smile for joy to see you suck my blood.

Lear. I am no cannibal that I should delight
To slake my hungry jaws with human flesh.
I am no devil or ten times worse than so
To suck the blood of such a peerless friend.
O, do not think that I respect my life
So dearly as I do thy loyal love.
Ah, Britain, I shall never see thee more,
That hast unkindly banishéd thy king.
And yet not thou dost make me to complain,
But they which were more near to me than thou.

It is at this point that they are discovered by Cordella, the Gallian King, and Mumford, who are disguised as country folk and are journeying among the peasantry. But before they reveal themselves, they listen to Leir tell his sad story of betrayal and his daughters' attempt on his life. The account so touches Cordella that she instantly forgives her father, and they spend several minutes kneeling to each other and asking each other's blessing.

The most important difference between *Leir* and *Lear*, however, is Shakespeare's introduction of a parallel plot, the Gloucester story. For this he went to a different source, Sir Philip Sidney's *The Countess of Pembroke's Arcadia* (1590), and the story of the Paphlagonian King and his two sons, Leonatus and Plexirtus. As Sidney presents it, the story begins in medias res, that is, after the king has been blinded. In his despair, he is ministered to by his legitimate good son, Leonatus, who earlier had been the victim of both his father's and his bastard half-brother's treachery. The king has wished to be led to a cliff to end his life in suicide, but Leonatus prevents him. It is now that they meet the two princes, Pyrocles and Musidorus, to whom they tell their story. The king tells them how Plexirtus had deceived "through poisonous hypocrisy, desperate fraud, smooth malice, hidden ambition, and smiling envy" to try to kill Leonatus, who fortunately escapes his wrath. Meanwhile, the king increasingly turns more and more responsibility over to Plexirtus until he was left "nothing but the name of a king." Finally, Plexirtus rids the king of even that, puts out his eyes, and instead of imprisoning or killing his father, delights rather in letting him feel his misery, wretchedness, and disgrace. It is then that Leonatus discovers his father and succors him, and Pyrocles and Musidorus find them.

The story continues as Plexirtus arrives with a band of men intent on killing his brother; but in the ensuing conflict, in which the two princes also take part, further rescue comes at the hands of some of their friends, Leonatus fights valiantly and is saved, while Plexirtus escapes. Returning to his kingdom, which Plexirtus has abandoned, the old blind king crowns his son Leonatus and then dies, "his heart broken with unkindness and affliction, stretched so far beyond his limits with this excess of comfort, as it were able no longer to keep safe his royal spirits." Shakespeare does not continue the story beyond this point, although Sidney goes on to show how Plexirtus returns with a rope around his neck to beg forgiveness of his brother, who, as always, generous and kind, grants him amnesty on the promise that he will amend his life.

In adapting this part of Sidney's *Arcadia*, Shakespeare made several important changes and embellishments. He shows just how Edmond succeeds in deceiving his father and his brother as well; but, unlike Sidney, he has Edgar assume the disguise of Tom o'Bedlam. He retains the abortive suicide attempt, but he alters the aftermath by having Edgar face Edmond in single combat and fatally wound him. Elsewhere in the *Arcadia*, Shakespeare may have gleaned some hints for other aspects of his play. For example, Queen Andromana's lust for the princes, Musidorus and Pyrocles, in chapter 20 may have suggested to the playwright Gonerill's and Regan's lust for Edmond, and her death by stabbing herself after her son is killed may have inspired Gonerill's suicide after Edmond is killed. The story of Plangus, the king of Iberia, in chapter 15, may have suggested the way Edmond deceives his father in 1.2. Other incidents, such as the storm in chapter 7 and the despairing thoughts in the verse of Plangus and Basilius in chapter 12, may have also set Shakespeare's imagination to work. Above all, Sidney's *Arcadia* very likely showed Shakespeare how to transform his sources in *King Lear* into the form of tragedy.

These are the principal sources of *King Lear*. A fuller account of Shakespeare's borrowing would have to include the influence of his reading in other works, such as Erasmus's *Praise of Folly*, for the role of the Fool and the thematic development of reason and madness. The Book of Job in the Old Testament provides parallels to the trials and tribulations endured by both Lear and Gloucester, and Revelation may have prompted apocalyptic allusions in the play.[12] Susan Snyder has drawn an interesting analogue to Shakespeare's play in the story of the Prodigal Son from the New Testament.[13] *King Lear* and the old play *Gorboduc* share numerous parallels; so do *King Lear* and *Selimus*, particularly as regards plot structure.[14]

Because no collections of folktales from the Elizabethan period survive, if indeed any were made, we cannot trace Shakespeare's debts to the story of Cinderella, which is closely analogous to Cordelia's experience in 1.1, or to other folk tales and folklore that Shakespeare may have borne in mind, consciously or unconsciously, as he wrote *King Lear*. Nevertheless, in "The Artist Exploring the Primitive: *King Lear*," F. D. Hoeniger argues that long before Shakespeare read printed accounts of the reign of King Leir, he may have heard about the king and his three daughters as a boy at his mother's or grandmother's knee, or from a schoolmaster. For the story by no means originates with Geoffrey of Monmouth, who simply wrote down what had been passed down from generation to generation, as similar legends are known to circulate elsewhere, for example in Corsica, Sicily, and Latin America. "What matters," Hoeniger says, "is not whether Shakespeare became first acquainted with [a particular folktale version] or one closer to Holinshed's chronicle, but that he thought of the story as an old tale of the folk about primitive Britain."[15] It is this primitivism, not merely in the setting but also in the origin of the Lear story, that must have appealed most strongly to Shakespeare, who reinforced the elements of primitivism he found in the legend in a variety of ways, for example by bringing the characters very close to nature.[16] Edgar's disguise as mad Tom is simultaneously a descent into the most basic aspects of human nature, as Lear recognizes in act 3 when he says, "Thou art the thing itself. . . . Unaccommodated man" (3.4.95). Tearing off his clothes, Lear rejects the "sophistication" of civilization and himself follows Edgar, his "Noble philosopher" (3.4.156), into a direct confrontation, or merging, with basic humanity and madness.

Hoeniger's point is a valid one. Though scholars constantly comb through the annals of history and literature to discover written sources for Shakespeare's plays, we need to remember that, while Shakespeare undoubtedly read widely, he also learned from others in conversation and through experience. His mind worked like a sponge, absorbing everything it came across, and then his imagination coupled with his fine sense of poetic drama transformed it into something else, something new and wonderful. This something became what we now call the Shakespeare canon.

NOTES

1. See Park Honan, *Shakespeare: A Life* (Oxford: Oxford University Press, 1998), pp. 225–29.

2. See Willard Farnham, *Shakespeare's Tragic Frontier* (Berkeley: University of California Press, 1950).

3. *Hamlet*, 3.4.159.

4. Jay L. Halio, "Hamlet's Alternatives," *Texas Studies in Literature and Language* 8 (1966), 169–88.

5. See "The Two Parts of 'Othello,' " *Shakespeare Survey* 21 (1968), 13–29.

6. See A. C. Bradley, "*Coriolanus*," in *Lectures on Poetry* (London: Macmillan, 1909), and Jay L. Halio, "*Coriolanus*: Shakespeare's 'Drama of Reconciliation,' " *Shakespeare Studies* 6 (1972), 289–303.

7. David Harris Willson, *A History of England* (New York: Holt, Rinehart and Winston, 1967), p. 357.

8. Ibid., p. 364.

9. Ibid., pp. 363–64.

10. See Kenneth Muir, "Samuel Harsnett and *King Lear*," *Review of English Studies* 2 (1951), 11–21, and Geoffrey Bullough, *Narrative and Dramatic Sources of Shakespeare's Plays*, 8 vols. (New York: Columbia University Press, 1957–75), VII (1973), 299 ff. Frank Brownlow has produced a modern edition of Harsnett's *Declaration*, published by the University of Delaware Press, 1993, in which Edgar's language can be traced very conveniently. Brownlow suggests that, as Bishop of Chichester, Vice-Chancellor of Cambridge University, and master of Pembroke College, Harsnett may have been among the audience in James's court on St. Stephen's Day, 1607.

11. Bullough, p. 273. Shakespeare, of course, could read Latin from his boyhood training at school.

12. See John Holloway, *The Story of the Night* (1981), p. 89, and Joseph Wittreich, "*Image of that Horror*": History, Prophecy, and Apocalypse in "King Lear" (San Marino, Calif.: Huntington Library, 1984), p. 26.

13. "*King Lear* and the Prodigal Son," *Shakespeare Quarterly* 17 (1966), 361–69.

14. Barbara Heliodora Carneiro de Mendonça, "The Influences of *Gorboduc* on *King Lear*," *Shakespeare Survey* 13 (1960), 41–48, and Inga-Stina Ewbank, "*King Lear* and *Selimus*," *Notes and Queries*, n.s., 4 (1957), 193–94. See also

Arthur F. Kinney, "Some Conjectures on the Composition of *King Lear*," *Shakespeare Survey* 33 (1980), 13–25.

15. F. D. Hoeniger, "The Artist Exploring the Primitive: *King Lear*," in *Some Facets of* King Lear: *Essays in Prismatic Criticism*, ed. Rosalie L. Colie and F. T. Flahiff (Toronto: University of Toronto Press, 1974); reprinted in *Critical Essays on Shakespeare's "King Lear,"* ed. Jay L. Halio (New York: G. K. Hall, 1996), p. 77.

16. Ibid., pp. 77–78.

3

DRAMATIC STRUCTURE

Among all of his tragedies, Shakespeare's *King Lear* has the most fully developed double plot. Rudimentary or abbreviated subplots appear in *Hamlet*, in Fortinbras's plot to invade Denmark, and in *Macbeth*, in Cawdor's treason and punishment. Nothing so extensive and complete as the Lear-Gloucester double plot appears elsewhere, except in the comedies and histories. There Shakespeare masterfully used his dramatic ability to employ multiple plots, for example, in *The Merchant of Venice* and *Much Ado about Nothing* among the comedies, and the Falstaff episodes in the two parts of *Henry IV*. It is unlikely, however, that in most of his tragedies Shakespeare was following classical examples and limiting his tragedies to a single main plot. For one thing, his plays are much longer than classical models; for another, they do not follow the unities of time and place. He probably did not know Greek tragedy and may only have learned of Aristotle's *Poetics* (if he did) indirectly. No; instinct may have prompted him more than anything else to concentrate the action on a single plot in the majority of his tragedies. If so, why, then, did he decide to introduce two fully developed plots in *King Lear*?

We shall never know the answer to that question with any certainty, for Shakespeare left no clues, and he is not around to interview. Some critics believe he used the Gloucester plot to universalize his theme; others, to contrast Lear's reaction to his fate with Gloucester's. Both old men suffer miserably at the hands of their wicked children, and both are ministered to by their more caring children. But both react in quite opposite ways to their experience.

Things move swiftly in *King Lear*. The so-called Cinderella story ends as quickly as it begins in the first scene, when Cordelia is banished from Lear's kingdom, deprived of a dowry and of any vestige of her father's favor. Her Prince Charming in the person of the King of France, unlike the Duke of Burgundy, recognizes her inherent value: "She is herself a dowry," he says (1.1.236), and makes her "queen of us, of ours, and our fair France" (252). After her farewell to her sisters, he takes Cordelia off to France, and she does not reappear until act 4. There she returns Britain to rescue Lear from the evil actions of her sisters, who start planning their moves against their father as soon as they have been given their shares of the kingdom (1.1.277–98).

In the Gloucester plot, which begins in the very next scene, things also move quickly. Edmond loses no time putting his plan into action to usurp Edgar's legacy by fomenting trouble between his father and half-brother. His plot is simple: to incite Gloucester against Edgar with a forged letter purporting to enlist his aid against their father and (like Gonerill and Regan) divide up the spoils. Using the most effective kind of psychology—of reluctantly showing Gloucester the letter he pretends to hide, and then weakly trying to extenuate Edgar's supposed villainy— Edmond succeeds in getting Gloucester to fall into his trap. His next move necessarily gets Edgar out of the way, and he succeeds brilliantly. Important to his plan is that father and son, Gloucester and Edgar, should not once confront each other about the alleged criminal action that Edmond attributes to Edgar. Edmond even goes so far in a later scene (2.1) to wound himself in a pretended defence against Edgar's alleged violence, all of which further enrages Gloucester.

No sooner is Cordelia out of the way in far-off France than Gonerill puts her plan into action to strip Lear of what little power he has left. She informs Oswald, her steward, in 1.3 to treat Lear with little or no respect so as to provoke an incident that will give her the opportunity she seeks to deal with him as she wants. Oswald immediately carries out his mistress's order and in 1.4, accordingly, upsets Lear. Meanwhile, Kent, who has interposed on Cordelia's behalf in the opening scene and whom Lear has banished for his pains, has returned in disguise to serve his old master. By tripping Oswald up and scolding him, he wins Lear's favor and assumes a place as his servant. Kent remains with Lear to the end of the play, not dropping his disguise before the old king until the last moments of Lear's life. But by then, it is too late; Lear never makes the connection between Kent and his servant Caius.

Both Gonerill and Regan, on the one hand, and Edmond on the other, move to isolate their fathers as far as possible. By the end of act 1, Lear has cursed Gonerill, who has refused to entertain his entire retinue of a hundred knights, and departs from her in anger. He flies to Regan, mistakenly believing that he has one daughter left who will treat him properly (1.4.210), and therefore fails to heed the Fool's slightly cryptic warning (1.5.11–15). He is unaware, of course, that Gonerill and Regan are working in concert and that Gonerill has alerted Regan of Lear's departure for her palace. In anticipation of that event, Regan cleverly arranges with her husband, Cornwall, to be absent from home and goes to Gloucester's castle instead. Why she should choose to go there is unclear, except that it provides her with an excuse later to urge Lear to return home with Gonerill (2.4.196). Dramatically, it enables Shakespeare to get the principal characters in the same place at the same time so that the final confrontation between Lear and his daughters can occur.

Regan and Cornwall's move to Gloucester's castle also sets up the events in the second plot that are of the utmost importance. Whereas Gloucester has appeared weak and vacillating through the end of act 2, he begins to assert himself quietly as a supporter of the king and against his daughters' treatment of him. Still convinced that Edmond is his true and loyal son, in 3.3 he confides in him that he means to succor Lear. He also says that he has received a letter from those promising to assist the king. The letter is presumably from Cordelia, but how he got it or how Cordelia has learned of events relating to her father is not explained. (In the theater we do not stop to ask such questions, as the action moves relentlessly forward.) This confidence leads to Gloucester's undoing, as Edmond promptly informs against him to Cornwall. The duke then determines to act against Gloucester as a traitor (3.5).

So far, the two plots have moved forward in parallel fashion. By the end of act 2, Lear has seen clearly how his elder daughters regard him and, stung by their ingratitude—and worse—he runs out into a storm that has been gathering momentum, accompanied only by the Fool and, soon after, Kent. While Lear rushes around out-of-doors exposed to the elements, he hurls defiance at the storm: "Blow, winds, crack your cheeks," he cries: "spit, fire; spout, rain!" (3.2.1–13). In his monomania, he connects the raging elements with his daughters:

> Nor rain, wind, thunder, fire are my daughters.
> I tax not you, you elements, with unkindness.
> I never gave you kingdom, called you children.
> You owe me no subscription. Then let fall
> Your horrible pleasure. Here I stand your slave,

A poor, infirm, weak, and despised old man.
But yet I call you servile ministers,
That will with two pernicious daughters join
Your high-engendered battles 'gainst a head
So old and white as this. O, ho! 'tis foul. (3.2.14–24)

Shortly afterwards, despite the self-pity that he continues to feel, or rather overriding it, he shouts (in a line only in the Folio), "Pour on, I will endure" (3.4.18).

Act 3 marks the change that begins to come over King Lear as he realizes more and more clearly the error of his ways. If the recognition helps drive him over the edge into madness, he later recovers under the ministering hand of his beloved Cordelia. But first he must undergo the purgatory of insanity, abetted unwittingly by his meeting with Edgar as Tom o'Bedlam. As Lear plunges deeper and deeper into madness, despite Kent's efforts and the Fool's to comfort him, he holds a trial of his daughters. For reasons best known to Shakespeare and/or his fellow players in the King's Men, this mock trial in part of 3.6 was cut from the Folio version of the play, but it is seldom omitted from modern productions, as it is extremely effective on stage.[1] Moreover, its juxtaposition with Gloucester's trial in the very next scene makes a decided point. By contrast with Lear's mad prosecution of his daughters, Cornwall and Regan's trial of Gloucester is a much greater mockery and madness. As for the travesty of justice it represents, Cornwall admits as much when he says:

Though well we may not pass upon his life
Without the form of justice, yet our power
Shall do a curtsy to our wrath, which men
May blame but not control. (3.7.24–27)

Having sent Edmond with Gonerill back to Albany, ominously indicating that "The revenges we are about to take upon your traitorous father are not fit for your beholding" (3.7.7–8), Cornwall then proceeds with Regan to accuse Gloucester of his "treachery" and to deal with it arbitrarily and ferociously.

Gloucester's reaction to his fate contrasts markedly with Lear's. While he reveals an even stronger measure of self-pity than Lear, his recourse—unlike Lear's—is to utter despair. Trapped by Edmond's treachery as he tries to assist the king and arranges for his conveyance to Dover, where

Cordelia lands with her army, Gloucester is pinioned by Cornwall's servants and tried for treason, while Regan insults him by plucking his beard. Astonished by this behavior of the duke, his "worthy arch and patron" (2.1.58), and his lady—in his own house, too, where they are his guests—Gloucester at first tries to extenuate. Then, recognizing what is happening, he submits with some show of defiance, but not for long. Asked why he has sent the king to Dover, he tells Regan:

> Because I would not see thy cruel nails
> Pluck out his poor old eyes, nor thy fierce sister
> In his anointed flesh stick boarish fangs. (3.7.55–57)

These words seal his fate, as Cornwall plucks out first one of his eyes and then, despite being wounded by a servant, the other. At this precise moment Gloucester learns that it was Edmond who informed against him (87–88), and he at last knows how terribly he has been deceived.

If Lear is filled with defiance and a determination to endure, to bring his daughters to justice and take vengeance against them, Gloucester behaves differently. Blinded, he now sees better, which is one of the compelling ironies (among many) in this tragedy. When an old man tries to lead him on his way outside his castle, from which he has been unceremoniously hurled, he says, "I have no way, and therefore want no eyes: / I stumbled when I saw" (4.1.18–19). To this extent Gloucester has gained some insight into himself. He does not yet understand, however, that he has much more to learn, which becomes Edgar's new role to teach him. For the present, Gloucester is determined to end his life by suicide and asks a poor beggar, Tom o'Bedlam, to lead him to Dover Cliffs to do it. There he again meets Lear, now utterly mad, who nevertheless preaches words of wisdom to him in one of the most poignant scenes of any drama.

Though Edgar is gone from the action after his soliloquy in 2.3, he returns in the middle of act 3 in the disguise he has assumed. His ravings as Poor Tom o'Bedlam help to develop the theme of madness versus reason, but they serve a dramatic function as well. Three forms of reason in madness are contrasted with each other in this central act: the assumed madness of Edgar as Tom, the Fool's nonsensical speech, and Lear's growing lunacy. While the Fool desperately tries to keep up with what is happening and contributes as much as he can to Tom's mad babble, by now he is utterly worn out and soon disappears altogether from the play. His place is taken over momentarily by Edgar in his role of Tom o'Bedlam and later by Lear on Dover Beach. Moreover, his ministry to Lear in the latter part of the play is assumed by Cordelia after her return to Britain in act 4. (Very likely the actor who played the Fool doubled as Cordelia.) What happens to the Fool as a character is never revealed, for Lear's line near the end, "And my poor fool is hanged" (5.3.279), is ambiguous. It refers probably to Cordelia but may possibly refer to the Fool.[2]

Lear also disappears from the action after act 3, to return again fully mad several scenes later at Dover Beach.[3] The dramatic action now turns instead to events involving others. In 4.1, Edgar, still in disguise as Tom, finds his blinded father and determines to help relieve his despair. Thus his ministry to his father begins, and ends only with Gloucester's death, reported by Edgar at 5.3.172–90. His action in helping restore his father to a better outlook on life parallels Cordelia's efforts to restore Lear to some semblance of sanity. Edgar's actions are both direct and indirect; all of Cordelia's are aimed directly at her father.

Meanwhile, the Duke of Albany reappears for the first time since the first act in 4.2, now quite altered in attitude toward his wife Gonerill and toward his sister-in-law Regan. Unsure earlier about their treatment of Lear (1.4.299–300), he now has no doubts about their villainy and up-braids Gonerill severely. But he is, as yet, unaware just how far his wife has betrayed his trust, for Gonerill has entered into an amorous relation-ship with Edmond, whom she now seriously desires for her mate. So does Regan, whose husband has died, killed by one of his servants trying to prevent him from totally blinding Gloucester. The rivalry between the two sisters heats up throughout this act and into the next, until Gonerill, seeing Regan's advantage over her as a widow while her husband still lives, poisons her sister. The lust for power that has motivated each of the elder daughters from the start here turns in upon itself.[4]

Cordelia's return to England is heralded by a scene between Kent and the Gentleman in act 4, which the Folio omits entirely. The reason for this omission is easy enough to discern. While the scene is filled with beautiful lyric poetry in which Cordelia is described in the most poignant terms, it does nothing to move forward the dramatic action of the play. Its omission on stage in modern productions is therefore seldom missed, the outcry of literary critics notwithstanding. Cordelia appears in the following scene, and the audience can see for itself what she is like, making the Gentleman's description of her more or less superfluous.

In her reappearance on British soil, Cordelia's primary concern is with her father, not conquering the realm, and she takes immediate steps to find and care for him (see 4.3.23–28).[5] In this effort, she does not succeed until the last scene of act 4, one of the most moving in the play and in all of Shakespeare's works. Whereas Edgar keeps his identity hidden from his father until the very end, Cordelia greets her father as herself and as gently and compassionately as possible. Perhaps it is because Shakespeare wished to make this scene stand out, and not dilute it with a comparable scene between Gloucester and Edgar, that Gloucester's reconciliation with his son is only reported, not dramatized (5.3.172–90).

Kent, who also appears in this scene of reconciliation at the end of act 4, refuses to drop his disguise before Lear, rejecting Cordelia's entreaties to him to do so. Apparently, he wants Lear finally to connect his services as Caius throughout the play with his true identity as the banished Kent. Although in the final scene Lear recognizes Kent for who he is, he never makes the connection between Caius and Kent. Kent, therefore, is deprived of the one reward he seems to have desired before any other. His disappointment and impending demise thus add to the ultimate impact of the tragedy.

All of the action of the drama from the last two scenes of act 3 has been building toward the climax in act 5. At the beginning of 5.1, the forces opposing Cordelia and Lear assemble, and this involves the co-alescence of characters from both plots. Edmond is now the earl of Gloucester, supplanting his father by Cornwall's order (3.5.14), and joins with Albany as a leader of the British forces. Gonerill and Regan vie for his favor, and, after the battle is won, Regan declares that he is tantamount to being her husband: "In my rights, / By me invested, he compeers the best" (5.3.62–63). As for Edmond, his dilemma is acute. He has played both sides of the street, so to speak, and is unsure how to resolve matters. As he states in his soliloquy at the end of 5.1:

> To both these sisters have I sworn my love,
> Each jealous of the other as the stung
> Are of the adder. Which of them shall I take?
> Both? one? or neither? Neither can be enjoyed
> If both remain alive. To take the widow
> Exasperates, makes mad her sister Gonerill,
> And hardly shall I carry out my side,
> Her husband being alive. Now then, we'll use
> His countenance for the battle, which being done,
> Let her who would be rid of him devise
> His speedy taking off. (5.1.44–54)

In this way, as in others, the two plots merge. The unanticipated resolution of the part of the action occurs after the battle when Edgar, as Albany's challenger against Edmond, defeats his brother in the duel and Gonerill, having poisoned Regan, commits suicide after seeing her lover fatally wounded.

But what of the action regarding Lear and Gloucester themselves? Once united with his blinded father, Edgar leads him to Dover but deceives him in his attempt to fling himself off a cliff. His device works and begins to extract Gloucester from despair. "Thy life's a miracle," he proclaims (4.5.55), and he gets Gloucester to accept this truth. Though he tends to backslide again into despair, Edgar keeps bringing him back from the slough of despondency, especially after the battle between Cordelia's forces and her sisters' ends in Cordelia's defeat. Only when he is about to meet Edmond in the duel does Edgar finally reveal himself to his father, desiring his blessing. The revelation causes the weak old man to succumb at last to death, caught between the conflicting passions of joy and grief (5.3.170–90).

The reason that Shakespeare does not dramatize this incident has been explained above. What requires explanation now is why, all along the way, Shakespeare repeatedly suggests the possibility of a happier outcome than he provides for the Lear plot. As early as the end of 2.2, for example, when Kent in the stocks reads a letter from Cordelia, we are led to hope that, between the two of them, Lear will be rescued and replaced on his throne. Similarly, in 3.3, when Gloucester tells Edmond of the letter he has received, these hopes are reinforced. Again, at 4.5.235–66, Edgar kills Oswald and takes from him the letter Gonerill has sent to Edmond and later delivers it instead to Albany, thus arousing expectation that the wickedness these characters have plotted will at last be undone. Finally, when the battle is lost but Edgar defeats Edmond in a duel, some hope remains when Edmond declares, "Some good I mean to do, / Despite of mine own nature" (5.3.217–18), and he discloses his plan to have Lear and Cordelia executed. Albany and Edgar send someone with Edmond's sword to the captain designated to carry out the hangings, and still we are allowed to believe the rescue will come in time. But it does not.

Why does Shakespeare disappoint expectation in this way? Perhaps it is because he wants the tragic experience to penetrate ever more deeply. In altering the ending from his sources, in which Lear is saved and restored to his throne by Cordelia, and which many in his audience (unlike those today) would have remembered, he provides a far more powerful ending. Nevertheless, for many years—over a century and a half, from the date of Nahum Tate's redaction in 1681 until Macready's restoration of Shakespeare's text in the mid-nineteenth century—the play did end happily during its life on the stage. True, eighteenth-century editors continued to supply readers with Shakespeare's original conclusion, even as a different version was enacted on the boards, as in David Garrick's famous representations.[6] Nevertheless, Samuel Johnson confessed that he could not bear to read Shakespeare's ending until he was forced to revise the play for his edition. And at least one major modern critic, Stephen Booth, has confessed to the same emotional reaction.[7]

The double plot Shakespeare uses in *King Lear* does more than universalize his themes, although it certainly does that. It also distinguishes among various kinds of good and evil and a human being's possible responses to them. By connecting the two plots in the climactic series of events in act 5, Shakespeare further heightens the dramatic effect of his tragedy, showing how evil embraces evil but ultimately does not prevail. True, it does considerable and dreadful damage, and many deplore the death of Cordelia, whose only fault was her stubborn honesty when speaking truthfully in 1.1. But in tragedy the innocent as well as the wicked suffer, and they suffer extremely. Ophelia, Desdemona, Lady Macduff and her children are further testimony to this tragic fact. Beyond the world of drama, unfortunately, we see this process enacted almost daily, as in recent instances of death and destruction among many innocent peoples worldwide. We cannot presume to account for tragedy by any rational process; but we can bear witness to it, as the survivors— Kent, Albany, and Edgar—do in *King Lear*.

NOTES

1. The omission involves some 30 lines following 3.6.14. See the appendix in the *New Cambridge* edition, pp. 297–99.

2. "Fool" was a common term of endearment in Shakespeare's time, but the word inevitably recalls the character of the Fool, not seen since 3.6. Moreover, if one actor played both Cordelia and the Fool, the ambiguity is reinforced.

3. Shakespeare often removes his main character from the action for a prolonged period of time to signal a significant change in that character, as he does for example in *Richard II* and *Hamlet*. Richard II is offstage from 2.2 to 3.2, and when he returns (from fighting against a rebellion in Ireland), he is a much more sympathetic person than he was before he left. Hamlet disappears from the action from 4.4 until 5.1, reentering Denmark from his aborted trip to En-

gland with a largely different attitude, more resigned now to accepting his role as "scourge and minister." In addition, Shakespeare usually has the character wear different clothes—Hamlet wrapped in his sea cloak, Lear no longer in the clothes he has ripped off in 3.4 (he is usually presented on stage fantastically decked out in 4.5 with flowers on his loose gown and a wreath of sorts on his head). Lear changes garments again in the final scene of act 4, when once again his personality alters.

4. In Q1 this is just as Albany predicts. If the heavens themselves do not intervene, he says, to stop the daughters from committing further "vile offences," then "Humanity must perforce prey upon itself / Like monsters of the deep." These lines appear in a long passage after 4.2.33 that the Folio text omits; see the New Cambridge edition, pp. 301–02, or any conflated edition of the play.

5. In conflated editions, these lines appear in 4.4.

6. See the chapter below on *King Lear* in performance.

7. Stephen Booth, *"King Lear," "Macbeth," Indefinition, and Tragedy* (New Haven: Yale University Press, 1983), p. 5.

4

THEMES

Like any Shakespeare play, *King Lear* has a variety of complex thematic developments. While some themes loom larger than others, no single theme dominates the whole. Among the major themes are: the division of the kingdom and its politics; the bonds between child and parent, parent and child, master and servant; social responsibility; the world of nature, including human nature; reason and madness. Many of the themes are interrelated, though for simplicity's sake and clarity of presentation, they will be treated separately as far as it is possible to do so.

THE DIVISION OF THE KINGDOMS

When James I succeeded Elizabeth I to the English throne in the spring of 1603, he was already a king, James VI of Scotland, a separate nation and for centuries an antagonist—often a violent one—to England. Many wars and skirmishes were fought along the border between the two countries, and the Scots seldom lost an opportunity, especially when England was at war with a European power, to invade their hated neighbors. James was determined to end this conflict. High on his initial agenda was uniting the two kingdoms into one, as Wales and England had been united much earlier. Unfortunately, it was to take a hundred years—well after the end of James's reign—before this ambition could be realized.

King Lear's announcement at the beginning of the play—that he intends to divide his kingdom into three parts—must therefore have struck a severely discordant note to Shakespeare's audience, especially when the play was performed at court. As most modern nations realize, in unity there is strength; in division, weakness abides. Why, then, does Lear make this apparently outlandish decision? He gives his reasons, more fully in the Folio than in the quarto text. He says that he is old and therefore wants to give up the responsibilities of kingship, although he wishes to retain the name and all the "additions," or titles and honors, of a king. Moreover, by dividing the kingdom now, he believes he will forestall the rivalry that might lead to "future strife" (1.1.32–40). He could not be more self-deceived, as events turn out; for, as Curran later informs Edmond (and the audience), conflict is soon brewing between the two dukes for control of the whole kingdom (2.1.6–13).[1]

Lear's most loyal retainers, those who stick by him through the worst of his experiences—Kent and the Fool—try to dissuade or enlighten the old man about the foolishness of his plan. For his pains, Kent is banished (1.1.157–75). Although he does not appear until after the decision has been implemented, the Fool harps on what he considers his master's madness, but to no avail. If the Fool's intention is to bring Lear back to his senses, he fails utterly. In fact, his efforts seem to have the opposite effect, for Lear plunges further and further into madness.

As the rivalry between Gonerill and Regan, Albany and Cornwall begins to heat up, another element in the political situation erupts. Hearing of her father's unfortunate situation, Cordelia pleads with her husband, the King of France, to intercede on Lear's behalf. This results in a foreign invasion by the French into England. Again, given the history of the antagonism between the two countries (although at the moment of performance in the early seventeenth century they were at peace), this incursion must have seemed especially disturbing to Shakespeare's audience. The deposition or death of a king—as Claudius notes in *Hamlet* (1.2.17–25)—rightly or wrongly leads its country's enemies to suspect a weakened government and a ripe opportunity for attack. This is not Cordelia's motive, of course: She explicitly states that she is not invading with a French army to conquer England, but to restore Lear to his rightful throne (4.23–29). Nevertheless, any English audience would be uncomfortable, not to say upset and antagonistic, at the very mention of a French invasion.

The disastrous result of Lear's decision to divide his realm is abundantly clear at the end. The country is in shambles. The entire royal family has been wiped out, and the survivors are thoroughly dejected. Albany no longer has the heart to rule and tries to turn over the reins of government to Kent and Edgar (another divided rule?). But Kent declines, aware that he will shortly follow his master Lear into death. Edgar, despite the maturity he has gained in the course of the play, is young and inexperienced, but nonetheless willing to accept Lear's legacy and repair the "gored state," all that is left of Britain.

BONDS BETWEEN PARENT AND CHILD, CHILD AND PARENT

When Lear proposes to his daughters that they tell him how much they love him, so that they can vie with each for the best part of the kingdom he is dividing among them, he has in fact already allocated the three parts of his realm. We learn as much from the opening dialogue between the earls of Gloucester and Kent (1.1.1–6). What prompts him to engage his children in this sham contest is evidently nothing more than vanity. Perhaps all three daughters recognize the contest for what it truly is, but Gonerill and Regan go along with the game anyway, professing in hyperbolic terms what they say they feel for their father. Cordelia refuses. In her asides to the audience she indicates her dilemma: "What shall Cordelia speak? Love, and be silent" (1.1.57). When Lear turns to her and asks what can she say to win "A third more opulent than your sisters," she replies simply, "Nothing, my lord" (1.1.82). Asked again, she reiterates her answer, to which Lear responds in a rage.

From one point of view, seldom remarked by commentators, Cordelia is absolutely right. Since the kingdom has already been divided up and two-thirds given away, only one third is left. Obviously, nothing she can say can get her more than what remains. But Lear is hardly in the mood for such logic, if even for a moment he recognizes that logic in Cordelia's reply. She can get nothing, of course, and that is precisely what she does get from her father for insisting on speaking the truth. But more inheres in the situation than that.

When explaining herself to Lear, Cordelia says she loves her father "According to my bond, no more nor less" (88). Lear takes this as an insult, particularly in the context of what Gonerill and Regan have just proclaimed. Cordelia is nevertheless correct in what she says, as she goes on to ask, "Why have my sisters husbands, if they say / They love you all?" (1.1.94–95). Again, Lear is in no mood for logic. He has been embarrassed in the open court and will not tolerate such behavior from his daughter—especially the one he has favored most. He then promptly disowns Cordelia and banishes her from his sight.

Along with later events, this incident brings sharply into focus the nature of the bond between parent and child, child and parent, and recalls a significant moment from an earlier Shakespearean play. When Desdemona is summoned before the court of Venice to explain her marriage to Othello, she also recognizes a divided loyalty between her father and her husband.[2] True, Cordelia does not yet have a husband. She will have one shortly before the scene ends, and she knows that the choice of a husband is the reason that the Duke of Burgundy and the King of France have been summoned before Lear.[3] The marriage ceremony and the Bible are quite specific, too, on the relation of children to parents after marriage.[4] A wedding does not sever the bond between parent and child, but it does seriously qualify it, as Cordelia fully understands, though not in the way Gonerill and Regan view the matter.

As the scene ends, Cordelia bids farewell to her sisters, recognizing the potential danger to her father, left in their hands. Gonerill and Regan, on their part, superciliously reject Cordelia's warning—"Prescribe us not our duty," Regan says (1.1.270). They then set about planning how to deal with the old king, their father. "We must do something, and i'th'heat," Gonerill tells Regan (298). And they do plenty.

Gonerill begins soon afterwards by stripping Lear of fifty of his hundred knights, the retinue he demanded as part of the settlement for dividing his kingdom between his daughters. Outraged, Lear curses Gonerill and flees to Regan, naively thinking that he will fare better with her. He is unaware that she and Gonerill are in cahoots, determined to deprive Lear of every shred of power, real or symbolic, he once had. When it comes down to it, they argue that he hardly needs a retinue of fifty, twenty-five, ten, or even five knights, since their own servants can supply his needs. "What need one?" Regan concludes (2.4.256).

In this way, Lear's elder daughters sever whatever bond they might have felt with their father. To Lear's plaintive cry, "I gave you all," Regan replies, "And in good time you gave it" (2.4.243). As they rationalize their position, Lear pleads, "O reason not the need. Our basest beggars / Are in the poorest thing superfluous" (257–58). He tries to argue that they are missing the point entirely. But he quickly breaks down and ends in incoherence, rushing out of the palace into the storm that has been brewing. Not that Gonerill, Regan, and Cornwall (who has been observing this all the while) care. " 'Tis his own blame," Gonerill says; "hath put himself from rest / And must needs taste his folly" (283–84). "Shut up your doors," Regan commands Gloucester. "He leads himself," Cornwall interjects. Whatever bond there once was between Lear's children and their father has completely evaporated.

But not where Cordelia is concerned. Hearing what has happened, she returns to England with an army hoping to set things right. Her effort costs her not less than everything, as she loses the battle and, because of Edmond's treachery, her life as well. But she has redeemed herself in her father's eyes, at least, and that, in the overall context of events, means more than anything else to him. When they are captured, Lear's only concern is that he may remain reunited with his beloved daughter. When Cordelia proposes that they see Gonerill and Regan, Lear rejects the suggestion: "No, no, no, no! Come, let's away to prison. / We two alone will sing like birds i'th'cage" (5.3.8–9). His happiness is complete, being with Cordelia in whatever conditions, even prison. Despite his rash action in scene 1, their bond has never really been broken. Certainly it has not for Cordelia, and perhaps not for Lear either. "I did her wrong," he says shortly after bad things begin to happen to him (1.5.20). Although the line is ambiguous—Lear could be referring to Gonerill whose palace he has just left—it more likely refers to Cordelia. In any event, their reconciliation at the end of act 4 is the most moving scene in all of Shakespeare, barring only the very last moments of this play.

In the parallel plot, that between Gloucester and his two sons, the bond between parent and child, child and parent, is also powerfully developed. If Lear is intemperate and rash, Gloucester is gullible and obtuse in his dealings with his sons. The net result is the same, however. In his soliloquy that opens 1.2, Edmond, like Gonerill and Regan, rationalizes his behavior. He dismisses as "the plague of custom" and "the curiosity of nations" the stigma he lies under as an illegitimate, younger son and determines to use his wits to deprive his half-brother Edgar of his inheritance. He fails to realize or refuses to accept what underlies society's predilection for first-born, legitimate children. It is not merely an arbitrary preference, but a deeply instinctual bond that leads parents to favor a first-born son and, as regards the rule of primogeniture, an intelligent custom as well.[5] In his locker-room conversation with Kent at the beginning of the play, when Gloucester describes Edmond's birth in Edmond's hearing, some critics discern a silent but outraged sensibility in the young man. Be that as it may, Gloucester, for better or worse, says he does not love Edmond any less than Edgar, even though Edmond, like many noblemen's children, has been educated not at home but elsewhere (most likely in another aristocrat's household).[6]

Edmond's plan to deceive both his father and brother works swiftly and effectively. One might question why Gloucester credits the forged letter Edmond pretends to hide from him. But then again, as another Shakespearen character says elsewhere, "It is a wise father that knows his own child" (*The Merchant of Venice*, 2.2.72). Gloucester apparently does not know either of his sons very well, and the bond between them cannot be very strong, or he could not be so easily taken in. But he is also the victim of an anxiety that will not let him rest in uncertainty. He thus jumps to the conclusion that Edmond has carefully prepared and calls Edgar "Abhorred villain, unnatural, destested, brutish villain—worse than brutish!" (1.2.69–70)—all this without for a moment confronting his son. But keeping father and son apart is very much a part of Edmond's plan, as he quickly gets Edgar to flee for his life (2.1.20–32).

Gloucester is distraught at these events, not only those that affect him directly, but others as well. In a choral comment bemoaning the evil influence of the heavens, he notes the severed bonds between friends, parents, children, and others:

> Love cools, friendship falls off, brothers divide. In cities, mutinies; in countries, discord; in palaces, treason; and the bond cracked 'twixt son and father. This villain of mine comes under the prediction: there's son against father. The king falls from bias of nature, there's father against child. . . . And the noble and true-hearted Kent banished; his offence, honesty. 'Tis strange. (1.2.94–103)

Strange indeed it is, but much stranger than Gloucester in his simplicity realizes. Stranger yet in this parallel plot are subsequent events. Given the chance, Edmond in act 3, scene 5 informs against his father, an act that leads directly to Gloucester's punishment—blinding—by Cornwall and Regan—and to the establishment of Edmond as the Earl of Gloucester in his father's place. But stranger still, though not if we consider Cordelia's comparable action, is Edgar's ministering to his father after he sees him blindly staggering about in 4.1.

Despite what happened earlier, which led him to assume the wretched guise of a madman beggar, Edgar still feels strongly bound to his father. He therefore does his utmost to succor him in his misery.

Some critics may regard Edgar as heartless because he delays revealing himself to Gloucester until act 5. But Edgar explains exactly what he is doing and why. The worst sin anyone can commit is the sin of despair, and Gloucester's despair when Edgar comes upon him in act 4 is total. Edgar thus feels he must help his father out of that despair, regardless of any other feelings he may have. It is a risky business, he realizes (4.5.41–45), as he leads Gloucester to what he pretends, and the old man believes, is the edge of a steep cliff near Dover Beach. But his plan does work. Assuming a new disguise, Edgar persuades Gloucester that he has indeed jumped off a high cliff and that his "life's a miracle" (4.5.55). Later, as Gloucester is in danger of relapsing into despair again after the defeat of Cordelia's forces, Edgar reminds him that all men "must endure / Their going hence even as their coming hither" (5.2.10). Only when he finally reveals himself does Gloucester's "flawed heart," caught between the extremes of joy and grief, "burst smilingly" (5.3.187– 190).

THE BONDS BETWEEN MASTER AND SERVANT

Other bonds besides those between parent and child, child and parent, are also important in *King Lear*. Chief among them is that which brings the Earl of Kent to serve Lear after he has been unceremoniously thrown out of the kingdom—banished on pain of his life never to return. But Kent does return, disguised as Caius, to continue serving his master. Lear does not recognize his former vassal—in Shakespearean drama, disguise is impenetrable—and thus asks this "stranger" who he is and why he wants to serve him. Their prose dialogue is instructive:

> *Lear* What art thou?
>
> *Kent* A very honest-hearted fellow and as poor as the king.
>
> *Lear* If thou be'st as poor for a subject as he's for a king, thou art poor enough. What wouldst thou?
>
> *Kent* Service.
>
> *Lear* Who wouldst thou serve?
>
> *Kent* You.
>
> *Lear* Dost thou know me, fellow?
>
> *Kent* No, sir, but you have that in your countenance which I would fain call master.
>
> *Lear* What's that?
>
> *Lear* Authority. (1.4.16–27)

Kent's testimony here is far from mere flattery. He means what he says, and it says much about King Lear that may otherwise be overlooked or underestimated. At least where Kent is concerned, nothing Lear does or has done can break the bond that holds the one to the other. As Lear's fortunes falter and fail, Kent remains with him to the end, even to the point where he indicates he will follow his master in death (5.3.295–96).

The Fool is another servant who does not betray his master, and his words on the subject are very much to the point. As he says (or sings) to Kent, finding him in the stocks:

> That sir which serves and seeks for gain
>   And follows but for form,
> Will pack when it begins to rain
>   And leave thee in the storm.
> But I will tarry, the fool will stay,
>   And let the wise man fly;
> The knave turns fool that runs away,
>   The fool no knave, perdy. (2.4.71–78)

Once the literal storm breaks (the Fool speaks metaphorically) and Lear runs out into it at the end of act 2, only the Fool and Kent are with him. None of the hundred knights—the "wise men" the Fool alludes to?—are anywhere in sight. Knaves they may be, but not Kent and not the Fool.[7]

Loyalty may of course be misplaced, and Shakespeare gives us the alternative version in the character of Oswald, Gonerill's steward. Loyal to the end, he is as bad as they come, for his loyalty is really a form of self-serving, contrasting directly with Kent's. This is the reason Kent denounces him at the beginning of 2.2. He knows Oswald for what he is and says as much. Edgar in his disguise as mad Tom o'Bedlam also provides some clues to the character of this despicable person when he describes the servant he himself claims to have been:

> A servingman, proud in heart and mind, that curled my hair, wore gloves in my cap, served the lust of my mistress' heart, and did the act of darkness with her. Swore as many oaths as I spake words, and broke them in the sweet face of heaven. One that slept in the contriving of lust and waked to do it. Wine loved I dearly, dice dearly, and in woman out-paramoured the Turk. False of heart, light of ear, bloody of hand; hog in sloth, fox in stealth, wolf in greediness, dog in madness, lion in prey. (3.4.77–85)

Whether Oswald is guilty of all of these sins, we cannot be sure. But he is guilty of some of them—whether he did the "act of darkness" with

Gonerill or not—for the description fits closely enough. Shakespeare does not insert such passages without reason.

Finally, one must take note of the nameless servants at the end of act 3 and especially the one who tries to prevent the Duke of Cornwall from blinding Gloucester's other eye. The time comes when loyalty to a master must give way to a higher loyalty—to morality, to decency. The First Servant says that he has served Cornwall ever since he was a child, but he never did better service than now to bid him hold his hand (3.7.71–74). When Cornwall refuses to desist, the man does the unheard of thing—he draws his sword against his master—only to be stabbed to death by Regan. Cornwall dies, too, but not before Shakespeare has established beyond question the limits of loyalty. The other two servants also indicate the measure of their service as (in the quarto version) they comment on the evil they have witnessed and determine to assist Gloucester in the best way they know how.

SOCIAL RESPONSIBILITY

Loyalty is not a one-way street. Issues of loyalty also involve issues of social responsibility, particularly the responsibility those in power have to those they govern—their loyalty to their subjects. If Lear shows irresponsibility in dividing up his kingdom, however well motivated he thought his decision was, he later learns not only how wrong he was, but also how he has neglected his obligations as king. Stripped of his power, out in the wild weather with only his Fool and Kent to help him in act 3, he is entreated to seek shelter in a poor hovel. At this point, something remarkable comes over him. For the first time, Lear begins to think of others' welfare besides his own.[8] When Kent urges him to enter the hovel, he replies: "Prithee, go in thyself, seek thine own ease" (3.4.23). A moment later, addressing the Fool, he says "In, boy, go first" (26). He then speaks what is for him an extraordinary prayer:

> Poor naked wretches, wheresoe'er you are
> That bide the pelting of this pitiless storm,
> How shall your houseless heads and unfed sides,
> Your looped and windowed raggedness defend you
> From seasons such as these? O I have ta'en
> Too little care of this. Take physic, pomp,
> Expose thyself to feel what wretches feel,

> That thou mayst shake the superflux to them
> And show the heavens more just. (3.4.28–36)

Lear's sense of social responsibility is here awakened as he realizes that, self-absorbed in his own affairs, he has been unmindful of the misery his subjects—or any rate the poorest among them—who were in his power to aid. Having taken "too little care of this," he says that others like himself (at least formerly) who have more than enough should undergo what the underprivileged poor feel, an experience that will prompt the rich to distribute their excessive wealth more equitably. By so doing, they will thereby "show the heavens more just" than they now appear.

Lear's speech in 3.4 follows from what he had begun to say at the end of 2.4, as Gonerill and Regan question his need to retain any number of knights. When Regan asks, "What need one," Lear replies:

> O reason not the need! Our basest beggars
> Are in the poorest thing superfluous.
> Allow not nature more than nature needs,
> Man's life is cheap as beast's. Thou art a lady;
> If only to go warm were gorgeous,
> Why nature needs not what thou gorgeous wear'st,
> Which scarcely keeps thee warm. But for true need—(2.4.257–63)

Lear cannot finish his speech, overcome as he is with passion and self-pity, but later, out in the storm, he realizes what true need truly is. The point is driven home most vividly when he confronts Edgar in the guise of Poor Tom, "unaccommodated man," and Lear begins to strip off his own clothes (3.4.91–97).[9]

Gloucester's experience relates closely to Lear's, as he too suffers extreme deprivation and torment. After being blinded, he begins to see things "feelingly" (4.5.143), having "stumbled" when he saw (4.1.19). At his request, the Old Man turns him over to the mad beggar, Poor Tom. It is Edgar in disguise, whom Gloucester asks to bring him to Dover, where he has sent the king. He gives Tom a purse of gold and echoes the sentiments we have heard Lear utter earlier:

> Here, take this purse, thou whom the heavens' plagues
> Have humbled to all strokes. That I am wretched
> Makes thee the happier. Heavens deal so still.
> Let the superfluous and lust-dieted man

That slaves your ordinance, that will not see
Because he does not feel, feel your power quickly.
So distribution should undo excess,
And each man have enough. (4.1.59–65)

In giving his purse to the beggar, Gloucester has begun to practice what
he preaches; moreover, by his action he unwittingly fulfills Lear's ex-
hortation in act 3. Shaking his "superflux" to the beggar Tom, he takes
the "physic," or medicine, that the king prescribes.

Albany, too, begins acting responsibly as joint ruler of half the kingdom of Britain. Convinced that Gonerill and Regan have acted criminally
in their abuse of power, he chastizes his wife for her brutal treatment of
her father and, upon hearing of what has happened to Gloucester, he
swears revenge upon the perpetrators of that gross injustice (4.2.63–65).
His feelings towards the daughters notwithstanding, Albany assumes his
proper role in protecting the kingdom against what is clearly a foreign
invasion. Urged by Edmond to prepare for battle, he says simply, using
the royal plural pronoun, "We will greet the time" (5.1.43). After the
British defeat the invading army, his actions show his continuing responsibility as, first, he asserts his superior position, demanding from
Edmond the captured prisoners. Then, armed with the letter Edgar has
given him, Albany confronts both his wife and her lover with their trea-
sonous behavior. Throughout the final scene he takes charge of events
despite the sisters' protestations, but at the end he willingly resigns his
power to the younger and presumably abler Edgar, his champion in the
duel with Edmond and the person now fitter than even he to rule the
"gored state" (5.3.294).

NATURE

As John F. Danby has written, "*King Lear* can be regarded as a play
dramatizing the meanings of the single word 'Nature.' "[10] It is, of course,
a play that dramatizes a good deal more than that, but the complex
significance of *nature*, which has a number of meanings in the play, is
extremely important. Here, the romantic concept of nature must not un-
duly influence our understanding. For Elizabethans, nature did not refer
to the Wordsworthian concept of a healing or beneficial aspect of creation, to which one might flee for recreation and restoration, for peace
and tranquility. For Shakespeare and his contemporaries, nature meant
"the visible creation regarded as an orderly arrangement."[11] Nature re-

ferred to something normative, a pattern of creation, reason displayed in nature and law as its innermost expression.[12] Self-restraint was important as the basis for the proper observance of law and custom, upon which law was largely founded in human society.

From the very outset of the play, *King Lear* explores many of these ideas, especially the ways in which nature, once violated, may become a terrible scourge. As Kent and Gloucester discuss the division of the kingdom in the opening dialogue, Edmond, Gloucester's bastard son, is present, and the discussion quickly turns to his birth and breeding. He is Gloucester's natural son and says little here, but his behavior later is anything but natural, both as regards his father and his half-brother, Edgar. When Lear enters and addresses his daughters, he asks:

> Which of you shall we say doth love us most,
> That we our largest bounty may extend
> Where nature doth with merit challenge? Gonerill,
> Our eldest born, speak first. (1.1.46–49)

In these words, Lear sets up a competition not only among his three daughters, but between "nature," or natural affection, and "merit," or deserving. Before the scene is over, we are aware of what a disastrous competition that is. On careful analysis, one sees how unnatural, because hyperbolical and hypocritical, the protestations of Gonerill and Regan are. Lear does not see this, although Cordelia and Kent do. Instead, Lear believes that Cordelia behaves unnaturally in refusing to say anything at first, and then responding quite properly how she loves and honors her father (1.1.90–98). For her honesty, Lear rewards her by denouncing her as his daughter and disowning her—a signal act against natural affection and family unity. And for their hollow protestations, Lear rewards Gonerill and Regan with everything he has, saving for himself only the "name and all th' addition to a king" (1.1.130), which he soon finds amounts to nothing of any substance.

In soliloquy at the beginning of the next scene, Edmond calls upon nature as his "goddess" (1.2.1) and proclaims that he is bound only to her law. His "Nature" is what in the nineteenth century the poet Alfred Lord Tennyson would describe as "Nature red in fang and claw"—the unbridled competition for survival of the fittest.[13] And Edmond here determines to prove himself more fit (and therefore, in his view, more deserving) than his legitimately born brother. He plays on the word "base" and its derivations, "bastard" and "baseness," wringing from them, as far as he can, any vestige of meaning, ridiculing, as he does so, not only these terms but also the "dull, stale, tired bed" where legitimate children are conceived. In "the lusty stealth of nature," he says, he and others like him "take / More composition and fierce quality" than "a whole tribe of fops," as he refers to the likes of Edgar. He questions, furthermore, why elder sons should have precedence over younger ones, for he is deprived on two counts: he is illegitimate, and he is Gloucester's second son. He dismisses the "curiosity of nations" that is the basis of primogeniture, the doctrine which decrees that the first-born son shall inherit, and he determines to challenge what he calls "the plague of custom." For a while he succeeds, almost totally, until more natural and reasonable forces prevail against him.

As Edmond's plot works, Gloucester comments on the unnatural events that have so far occurred, those affecting himself and those affecting others. "Though the wisdom of nature can reason it thus and thus," he says, "yet nature finds itself scourged by the sequent effects" (1.2.92–93). He uses "nature" in two senses: human nature, specifically human nature as embodied in natural philosophy, or science, and the whole world of nature, including human nature. He refers to the "late eclipses of the sun and moon," which he regards as ominous portents, and notes the unnatural disasters in the human realm that have followed: "Love cools, friendship falls off, brothers divide. In cities, mutinies; in countries, discord; in palaces, treason; and the bond cracked 'twixt son and father" (1.2.94–96). He goes on to enumerate more specifically the unnatural events, or "ruinous disorders," as he calls them; to which (after his father leaves) Edmond responds with derision, rejecting Gloucester's belief in "spherical predominance," or planetary influence, as mere superstition. He then begins to work on Edgar, a man "Whose nature is so far from doing harms / That he suspects none; on whose foolish honesty" (1.2.152–53) he plays easily. But it is Edgar's good nature, educated by the buffets and abuse he soon begins to experience, that triumphs in the end over Edmond.

Meanwhile, the effects of Lear's violations of nature begin to mount. Oswald's behavior to the king early in 1.4 is the first sign of disruption. When Gonerill confronts her father on the behavior of his knights, Lear is astonished at her speech and asks, "Are you our daughter?" (1.4.178). He cannot believe she speaks to him as she does. The Fool[14] comments on this perversion of nature when he says during this dialogue, "May not an ass know when the cart draws the horse?" (1.4.183).[15] Outraged at Gonerill's persistence in treating him disrespectfully, Lear calls her

"Degenerate bastard" (1.4.209) and cites her ingratitude as he prepares to leave her palace for Regan's. He now starts to recognize the folly he has let "in" and his dear judgement "out" (1.4.225–27), a perversion of natural reason. But he still has a good deal more to learn when he finally meets up with Regan and Cornwall and discovers, as the Fool had warned, that one daughter is very much like the other (1.5.11–12).

Lear's prayer to the goddess Nature at 1.4.230–44 contrasts with Edmond's in 1.2. The goddess he addresses is not the goddess of unbridled competition but that of procreation and reproduction. Cursing his daughter, he implores Nature to "suspend her purpose" if she intends to make Gonerill "fruitful," that is, bear children. If Gonerill has a child, he asks that it become "a thwart disnatured torment" to her as she has been to him. Lear no longer recognizes Gonerill as a human being. Having called her "Destested kite" (1.4.217), he now refers to her "wolvish visage" (1.4.263). But his encounter in the next act with Regan is even worse.

Finding Regan not at home, Lear has to follow her around the countryside at night until he finally catches up with her and Cornwall at Gloucester's palace. The first thing he sees there is Kent in the stocks, and he cannot believe that Regan and Cornwall would so insult him by treating his royal messenger in this manner: "They could not, would not do't," he cries. " 'Tis worse than murder, / To do upon respect such violent outrage" (2.4.20–21). The insult is compounded when his daughter and son-in-law refuse to speak with him, using lame excuses (2.4.81–82). When at last they do appear, Lear with difficulty tries to control himself as he recounts what Gonerill has done, but he receives little sympathy from Regan:

> O sir, you are old,
> Nature in you stands on the very verge
> Of his confine. You should be ruled and led
> By some discretion that discerns your state
> Better than you yourself. Therefore I pray you
> That to our sister you do make return;
> Say you have wronged her. (2.4.138–44)

Lear's response is to mimic a false repentance and then start cursing Gonerill once more. Regan has little patience with this behavior, and, hearing her father's curses, she says she fears he will curse her too "When the rash mood is on" (162). Lear reassures her on this count and says "Thy tender-hefted nature shall not give / Thee o'er to harshness" (164–65). How little he knows his daughters.

Within a few moments, Gonerill herself arrives, and Lear is shocked to see Regan take her by the hand. The two women combine to strip Lear of all of his knights and reduce him to complete dependence. Trying to reason with them, he says "Our basest beggars / Are in the poorest thing superfluous. / Allow not nature more than nature needs, / Man's life is cheap as beast's" (257–59). In other words, by reducing a person's needs to the lowest common denominator, one can no longer distinguish a human being from a beast. Calling his daughters "unnatural hags" (271), he breaks down almost completely and runs out into the storm that has been gathering while their contretemps has developed.

Apparently, Shakespeare and his contemporaries still clung to the traditional belief that all of nature, human and otherwise, is somehow connected and integrated in an orderly fashion. To disturb one part of that order inevitably causes disruption in other parts.[16] The unnatural behavior of his daughters to their father (also their king), upsetting the obedience and gratitude that children naturally owe their parents (as subjects owe their sovereign), is reflected in the storm that rages out-of-doors, a violent disturbance in the elements of non-human nature. Shakespeare elsewhere shows how this can happen once any part of the natural order is violated. In *A Midsummer Night's Dream*, for example, Titania's insubordination to her lord and master Oberon in refusing to surrender the little Indian prince has led, as she herself recognizes, to the confusion of the seasons and other disruptions in the natural world. Similarly, when Macbeth murders Duncan—not only his king, but also his kinsman and guest—an unnatural darkness covers Scotland, and in the animal kingdom a mousing owl (an inferior species of bird) attacks a falcon.[17] "Take but degree away, untune that string," Shakespeare's Ulysses says, "And hark what discord follows" (*Troilus and Cressida* 1.3.109–10).

Out in the storm, Lear now confronts the nonhuman elements, daring them to do their worst (3.2.1–9). In his increasing dementia, he believes the wind and the rain have conjoined as "servile ministers," or agents, with his daughters to afflict him with their fury (3.2.20–23). The storm is terrifying, as Kent says when he finds Lear:

> Since I was a man
> Such sheets of fire, such bursts of horrid thunder,
> Such groans of roaring wind and rain I never

Remember to have heard. Man's nature cannot carry
Th' affliction nor the fear. (3.2.43–47)

An ordinary man's nature may not be able to carry "Th'affliction nor
the fear," as Kent says, but Lear is no ordinary man. He defies the
elements, daring them to do their worst: "Pour on," he shouts, "I will
endure" (3.4.18).

While all this is going on and Lear is at length persuaded to seek
shelter, other unnatural events occur. No longer willing to stand idly by
and see what Gonerill, Regan, and Cornwall are doing, Gloucester resolves to help the king. Mistakenly he confides in his son:

Alack, alack, Edmond, I like not this unnatural dealing. When I
desired their leave that I might pity him, they took from me the use
of mine own house, charged me on pain of perpetual displeasure
neither to speak of him, entreat for him, or any way sustain him.
(3.3.1–5)

Edmond hypocritically replies, "Most savage and unnatural!" as indeed
it is. But worse follows, when Gloucester tells him of a letter he has
received concerning the power that is arriving to aid Lear and advises
Edmond that they must "incline to the king" (12). Warning that "There
is strange things toward" (16), Gloucester leaves Edmond, who then
reveals in soliloquy that he will inform against his father to the Duke of
Cornwall.

Edmond does so, again hypocritically lamenting to Cornwall, "How,
my lord, I may be censured, that nature thus gives way to loyalty, something fears me to think of" (3.5.2–3). His "loyalty" to the evil partners
moves him one more step up the ladder of power that he desires, but it
is a clear violation of nature, as he himself recognizes, to act as he does.
Then again, his devotion is not to normal human nature but to the goddess he proclaimed in 1.2. Further violations of normal human nature
ensue, when Cornwall sends for the "traitor" Gloucester (3.7.3) and Gonerill and Regan eagerly await his punishment:

Regan Hang him instantly.
Gonerill Pluck out his eyes. (3.7.4–5)

Cornwall has at least the decency to send Edmond away with Gonerill
so that he will not witness the cruel and inhuman treatment his father

receives. The vicious blinding of the old earl is relieved only by the insubordination of one of the servants, who rebels at this unnatural proceeding by his master, and whom Regan kills for his efforts.

Despite the injustice he has suffered at Gloucester's hands, when Edgar sees his father's deplorable condition in the next scene (4.1), his natural affection reasserts itself, and his ministry to him begins. Eventually, he drops his disguise as Tom o'Bedlam to assume other disguises more appropriate to the situation, refusing until the climactic events of act 5 to reveal himself to his father.[18] Cordelia, like Edgar, also reasserts her love and devotion to her father in this act and does everything she can to cure him of his illness. The Gentleman[19] advises her on the proper treatment:

> There is means, madam.
> Our foster-nurse of nature is repose,
> The which he lacks. That to provoke in him
> Are many simples operative, whose power
> Will close the eye of anguish. (4.3.11–15)

When Cordelia's soldiers finally catch Lear and bring him to Cordelia, where he receives the recommended treatment, he awakens from a profound and curative sleep for his reunion with her. The natural love between parent and child, father and daughter, overcoming all previous misadventure, is presented in one of the most touching scenes in Shakespeare (4.6).

As opposed to these scenes of natural human devotion, the rivalry between Gonerill and Regan for Edmond's affection breaks out furiously in act 5 and culminates in Regan's death at her sister's hands and Gonerill's suicide. A different rivalry between the brothers, Edgar and Edmond, also occurs in this act, although Edmond is not aware of his opponent's identity until after he is defeated in their duel. Unlike the sisters, these brothers reconcile after a fashion as they exchange charity (5.3.153–59). And after he hears Edgar's account of his experience as an assumed madman and of nursing his father (172–89), Edmond says it has moved him and "shall perchance do good" (190–91). But it is not until after the bodies of Gonerill and Regan are brought in and Kent enters inquiring after Lear, that Edmond says, "Some good I mean to do, / Despite of mine own nature" (217–18). The good he means to do is to reprieve Lear and Cordelia from the death sentences he has imposed, but the message arrives too late to save Cordelia. When he himself dies,

Albany remarks, as he watches Lear trying to revive Cordelia, the third of his dead daughters around him, "That's but a trifle here" (269). And so it is. Nature—the normative aspects of nature as Elizabethans regarded it—has been violated too often and too vehemently by this time for the good that Edmond or anyone else means to do. It remains for the next generation, under Edgar's leadership, to sustain the "gored state" and try to restore it to what once it might have been.

REASON AND MADNESS

Closely related to the theme of nature is the theme of reason and madness. If normative nature reflects the operation of reason, with law as its innermost expression, as noted above, then madness reflects nature disrupted, or reason perverted. Modern psychiatrists do not like to use the term "madness" or "insanity"; they prefer "mental illness." But the old-fashioned terms have their usefulness when discussing a play like *King Lear*, for they stand in clearer opposition to terms like "reason," "sense," or "sanity" than any others. In this play, more than in *Hamlet*, Shakespeare explores the relationship between reason and madness, sense and nonsense, in great depth. Various kinds of madness are contrasted with each other and all of them with commonly accepted modes of sanity. Edgar's assumed madness as he impersonates Tom o'Bedlam in act 3 stands in comparison with the genuine and extreme madness of King Lear in act 4. The rationalist discourses of Gonerill, Regan, and Edmond stand in comparison with the reasonableness of Cordelia and Kent. The Fool's utterance is a special case entirely. Speaking in apparent nonsense, he often makes the greatest sense of all, once we plumb beneath the surface silliness of his words. A good example is his dialogue with Lear in 1.5; another is his speech at the end of 3.2, "Merlin's Prophecy," unique to the Folio.[20]

Is Lear mad at the very beginning, or merely foolish, when he determines to divide up his kingdom among his daughters? When Kent tries to reason with him, he gets nowhere and blurts out in exasperation, "Be Kent unmannerly / When Lear is mad" (1.1.139–40). By this, Kent means that Lear is acting unwisely, not that he has gone out of his mind. But Lear does eventually go out of his mind, driven there not only by the treatment of his daughters, but as much or more by the growing recognition that he has indeed acted unwisely and unjustly and by his passionate reaction to this insight.

What finally tips Lear over the edge into madness, ironically, is the assumed madness of Edgar as Tom o'Bedlam, whom he encounters during the storm in act 3. He cannot believe that anything less than Tom's gift of everything to his daughters could bring him to the condition he sees. But Lear is still sane enough to realize in Tom's desperate condition the basic nature of humanity. "Is man no more than this?" he asks rhetorically, looking at Edgar's near naked body:

> Thou ow'st the worm no silk, the beast no hide, the sheep no wool, the cat no perfume. Ha! Here's three on's are sophisticated; thou art the thing itself. Unaccommodated man is no more but such a poor, bare, forked animal as thou art. (3.4.93–97)

In sympathy, Lear begins to tear off his own clothes, and in 3.6 he plunges headlong into lunacy, desperately attempting to hold a trial of Gonerill and Regan. He begins asking imponderable questions: "Is there any cause in nature that make these hard-hearts?" (3.6.34). Here his mad ravings carry an element of sense or wisdom that in his saner moments Lear seemed incapable of. His sense in nonsense appears again when he addresses Gloucester on Dover Beach:

> What, art mad? A man may see how this world goes with no eyes; look with thine ears. See how yond justice rails upon yond simple thief. Hark, in thine ear: change places, and handy dandy, which is the justice, which is the thief? (4.5.144–47)

Edgar's comment a few lines later epitomizes Lear's discourse:

> O matter and impertinency mixed,
> Reason in madness. (166–67)

Earlier, Edgar's assumed mad utterances, emulating as they do the ravings of those believed to be possessed by the devil, similarly convey elements of truth, however unpalatable. His description of himself as one of the poor Bedlam beggars that rove over the land could tear the heart out of anyone willing enough to listen:

> Who gives anything to Poor Tom, whom the foul fiend hath led through fire and through flame, through ford and whirlpool, o'er bog and quagmire; that hath laid knives under his pillow and halters in his pew; set ratsbane by his porridge; made him proud of heart to

ride on a bay trotting-horse over four-inched bridges, to course his own shadow for a traitor. (3.4.49–54)

The difference between Tom's madness and Lear's is not merely that one is assumed and the other real. Edgar's is that of someone driven by wickedness and paranoia; Lear's, of someone driven by shame and profound humiliation. Both are afflicted with a strong sense of sex-revulsion.

Unlike either Poor Tom or Lear in his madness, but related to both, is the Fool's nonsensical utterances. Gonerill refers to him as Lear's "all-licensed Fool" (1.4.160), that is, someone who, because of his mental condition, can get away with saying things that others cannot. He is an "allowed fool," though even he sometimes has to be cautioned against going too far when he says things that cut close to the bone (see 1.4.99, 142). His poems and songs are full of mother wit and wisdom that no one seems to heed, except perhaps Kent, who recognizes that "This is not altogether fool."[21] After Lear bursts out of Gonerill's palace intending to go to Regan's, the Fool tries to warn him against this new folly:

> Shalt see thy other daughter will use thee kindly; for though she's
> as like this as a crab's like an apple, yet I can tell what I can tell.
> (1.5.11–13)

Later, during the storm, he is the first to try to get Lear to come in out of the brutal weather that rages around him, but to no avail. He still utters his poems and songs, trying to cheer the old king up, but conveying more wisdom and wit than nonsense, as in:

> The codpiece that will house
> Before the head has any,
> The head and he shall louse;
> So beggars marry many.
> The man that makes his toe
> What he his heart should make,
> Shall of a corn cry woe,
> And turn his sleep to wake. (3.2.25–32)

But the Fool meets his match, or is perhaps overmatched, by Edgar as Tom o'Bedlam, and soon afterwards vanishes.

In striking contrast to these madmen and fools are the apparently sensible and rational characters, Edmond, Gonerill, and Regan. But as

Shakespeare develops these characters, he shows us that their rationalism is superficial; it is fed, or rather led, by lusts that are deeply irrational— the lust for power and the lust for sex. As a result, these characters are ultimately self-defeated. Not satisfied with gaining superiority over his brother Edgar, Edmond goes further, betrays his father, and then woos or allows himself to be wooed by both Gonerill and Regan, hoping to become supreme ruler of the land. He is thus a Renaissance overreacher, such as Christopher Marlowe loved to portray in dramas like *The Jew of Malta* and *Dr. Faustus*. His cool-sounding discourse is full of hypoc- risy, as when he informs against his father to Cornwall: "How malicious is my fortune, that I must repent to be just! . . . O heavens, that this treason were not, or not I the detector!" (3.5.7–10).

Gonerill's case against Lear in 1.4 is at best plausible, but only that. She complains to her father:

> Here do you keep a hundred knights and squires,
> Men so disordered, so deboshed and bold,
> That this our court, infected with their manners,
> Shows like a riotous inn; epicurism and lust
> Makes it more like a tavern or a brothel
> Than a graced palace. (1.4.196–201)

She may be right, although the only appearance of Lear's knights earlier in the scene (44–65) does not convey the impression she describes, if a single knight may be taken as representative of the whole. Still, one wonders how a housewife today might feel if her father, husband, or son brought home a platoon of his old combat buddies to spend a few weeks together in their house, regardless of how large it was.

Gonerill goes too far, however, along with Regan, and it soon becomes clear what they are really up to. Albany puts it in the proper perspective in act 4, when he sees what they have been doing:

> Tigers, not daughters, what have you performed?
> A father, and a gracious agèd man,
> Whose reverence even the head-lugged bear would lick,
> Most barbarous, most degenerate, have you madded.
> Could my good brother suffer you to do it?
> A man, a prince, by him so benefited?
> If that the heavens do not their visible spirits
> Send quickly down to tame these vilde offences,

It will come.
Humanity must perforce prey on itself,
Like monsters of the deep.[22]

Humanity like theirs—Gonerill's, Regan's, and Edmond's—does indeed
prey on itself, as the last act shows. But well before then we see how
for all their rationalism, these villains do not operate reasonably.

The clearest example occurs in 3.7, Gloucester's trial and blinding.
The cruelty of their treatment of the old earl reveals it is animal lust,
not reason, that motivates Gonerill, Cornwall, and Regan. Gonerill starts
off by demanding "Pluck out his eyes" (3.7.5)[23] as Edmond stands by,
and Cornwall and Regan follow through. When the scene ends, their
rationalism fails them, as Regan later recognizes when she learns that
the pitiful sight of blinded Gloucester stirs hearts against the rulers of
the realm while they prepare to meet the invading French army (4.4.11–
14). Likewise, Gonerill oversteps reason when she commits herself to
Edmond in a letter, entrusting it to Oswald, whom Edgar confronts and
slays. It is this letter that Edgar delivers not to Edmond, as Oswald
requested, but to Albany, who thereby learns of his wife's treasonable
behavior and Edmond's. He then deals with it accordingly in 5.3 after
the battle.

For the true voice of reason, we have to turn to others, to Cordelia,
Kent, Albany, and Edgar. Cordelia's behavior in the first scene has already been noted; so has Kent's. But these two later go beyond even
reason in their loyalty and service to Lear, risking their lives in the
process. (Recall the Fool's verses on the knave who runs away, 2.4.71–
78, cited above). Likewise, Edgar ministers to his father. He tells him,
rightly, "Thy life's a miracle" (4.5.55) and later, when Gloucester falls
back into despair, "Men must endure / Their going hence even as their
coming hither. / Ripeness is all" (5.2.9–11). He here invokes both Christian teaching and pagan (Stoic) ethic, both of which vehemently opposed
suicide on very reasonable grounds.[24]

Albany's early speeches are perhaps the most dispassionate and reasonable of all. At first, he tries to restrain his wife from acting as she
does against Lear: "Well, you may fear too far" (1.4.282). In response
to her argument of justification, he says, "How far your eyes may pierce
I cannot tell; / Striving to better, oft we mar what's well" (299–300).
Getting nowhere, he appears to reserve judgment: "Well, well th' event,"
he says (302). We do not see him again until 4.2, when he lets fly against
his wife (see above). A reasonable man, by then he has seen and heard

enough. But, under the threat of invasion, he must defer any action against her to deal with matters more pressing.

As matters grow to a dangerous head, Albany still manages to speak reasonably in greeting Regan and Edmond:

> Our very loving sister, well bemet.
> Sir, this I heard: the king is come to his daughter,
> With others whom the rigour of our state
> Forced to cry out. (5.1.15–18)[25]

The duke then calmly proposes to plan the battle with "th' ancient of war," that is, the experienced commanders in the field. Even after he receives the letter that Edgar has taken from Oswald, he keeps his cool, confronting Edmond and Gonerill after the battle with reasonable composure, but also with firmness and deliberateness. If he elsewhere appears weak or hesitant, at least in the Folio version of *King Lear*, he is not now, with reason and justice on his side. After Cordelia and Lear have died, however, he relinquishes the realm to those he feels may be more capable of ruling it. Reason mingled with compassion—the best kind of mixture, as events have shown—now speaks through him to those who survive, and to us.

The last lines of the play, which Q gives to Albany, are in F assigned to Edgar, who has earned the right to rule in Britain by what he has experienced and learned. By the same token, he has earned the right to speak last, once again with the voice of reason:

> The weight of this sad time we must obey,
> Speak what we feel, not what we ought to say.
> The oldest hath borne most; we that are young
> Shall never see so much, nor live so long. (5.3.297–300)

NOTES

1. Kent reiterates what Curran tells Edmond when he speaks with the Gentleman at 3.1.11–13.

2. See *Othello*, 1.3.179–88.

3. In one of Shakespeare's sources, the earlier play *King Leir*, the love-contest was not to divide up the kingdom but a stratagem to compel Cordella to accept Leir's choice of a husband for her.

4. See, for instance, Genesis 2.24, Matthew 19.5–6, and compare Naseeb

Shaheen, *Biblical References in Shakespeare's Tragedies* (Newark: University of Delaware Press, 1987), p. 147.

5. Under primogeniture, the eldest son inherited all the land his father owned, in this way preserving property intact—as opposed to repeated divisions that ultimately could result in tracts of land so small as to be no longer viable possessions.

6. This was common practice in Elizabethan England. One explanation for it is that it prevented parents from becoming too attached to their offspring at a time when infant and child mortality was rampant.

7. On the disappearance of the knights, see Bradley, *Shakespearean Tragedy*, 3rd ed. (London: Macmillan, 1992), Appendix, Note T. Bradley believes the Fool might be alluding to the missing knights in these lines and the lines immediately preceding. Alternatively, he suggests that, in Shakespeare's revision, something has dropped out that would explain their disappearance from the action. At 3.7.15–19, Oswald says that "Some five or six and thirty of his knights" have followed Lear and are accompanying him to Dover, but the knights never appear in any subsequent scene, unless they have merged with Cordelia's army that has landed at Dover, as well they might have done.

8. See 3.2.66–71, where Lear starts to show concern for his Fool, cold and shivering out in the wind and the rain.

9. The Russian director Grigori Kozintsev dramatized Lear's speech by showing not only Lear and his tiny entourage, but also scores of "poor wretches" in the shelter, which in his film was not a mere hovel. He made his film, of course, while the Soviet Union still existed and pursued its socialist policies. See the chapter below on the play in performance.

10. John F. Danby, *Shakespeare's Doctrine of Nature: A Study of* King Lear (London: Faber and Faber, 1948), p. 15.

11. Ibid.

12. Ibid., p. 21. On reason and madness, see the next section in this chapter.

13. For a detailed analysis of Edmond's concept of nature and the origins of his ideas, see W. R. Elton, *"King Lear" and the Gods* 2nd ed. (Lexington: University Press of Kentucky, 1988), pp. 125–35.

14. Although he is not specifically referred to as such in this play, Shakespeare's audience would recognize the Fool as a "natural," that is, an idiot or retarded person. He is therefore allowed to say whatever he wants; Gonerill refers to him as "all-licensed" (1.4.160). But this is one of Shakespeare's wise fools, compelled to speak the truth, no matter what the consequences (1.4.97–98). (See Enid Welsford, *The Fool: His Social and Literary History* [1935; rpt. Garden City, N.Y.: Doubleday, 1961]). He is anything but an idiot, despite his peculiar discourse. Shakespeare often plays upon the terms "fool" and "natural," as later when, in his madness, Lear refers to himself as the "natural fool of fortune" (4.5.183). Compare also *Twelfth Night*, 1.3.25–28.

15. The Fool often makes similar comments on perversions of nature. Compare, for example, 1.4.88–90, 1.4.133–35, 1.5.33–36.

16. For the clearest statement of this concept in Shakespeare, see Ulysses' great speech on "degree," or order, in *Troilus and Cressida* 1.3.77–137. Albany cites the disruptions in human nature when he scolds Gonerill in 4.2 (in lines found only in Q: see the New Cambridge edition, pp. 301–2.)

17. See *A Midsummer Night's Dream* 2.1.81–117; *Macbeth* 1.7.12–16, 2.4.1–18; and compare the events preceding the assassination of Caesar in *Julius Caesar* 1.3.32.

18. On Edgar and his ministry, and the reasons why he does not reveal himself to his father sooner, see the section on bonds between parents and children, above.

19. A "Doctor" in Q, in F he becomes a "Gentleman," probably a surgeon. The British call surgeons "Mr.", not "Dr.", even today. See Gary Taylor, "The war in *King Lear*," *Shakespeare Survey* 33 (1980), 30.

20. Some scholars regard these lines, garbled somewhat in the Folio, as spurious; but see the notes to 3.2.79–92 and 3.2.83–84 in the New Cambridge edition.

21. This line appears only in Q, several lines after 1.4.119. See the New Cambridge edition, p. 294, for the entire context, which includes some seventeen lines omitted in F, and pp. 266–67 for an explanation of the omission.

22. These lines appear only in Q, in a long passage following 4.2.33. (See note 16, above.) The omission in F may be the result of altering Albany's character, weakening it while strengthening Edgar's. It is one of a number of deletions from 3.6 onwards, where shortening was also a likely motive.

23. This is a curious demand as a punishment for treason and suggests something about Gonerill's vicious character. See my article, "Gloucester's Blinding," in *Shakespeare Quarterly* 43 (1992), 221–23.

24. On "Ripeness is all," see J. V. Cunningham, *Woe or Wonder: The Emotional Effect of Shakespearean Tragedy* (1951; reprint. Denver: Alan Swallow, 1964), pp. 7–13, and compare W. R. Elton, *"King Lear" and the Gods*, 2nd ed. (Lexington: University Press of Kentucky, 1988), pp. 99–107.

25. The Folio cuts the following lines, which appear only in Q, and which further indicate Albany's reasonable attitude:

> Where I could not be honest,
> I never yet was valiant. For this business,
> It touches us as France invades our land,
> Not bolds the king with others whom I fear
> Most just and heavy causes make oppose.

Even Edmond remarks that Albany "speaks nobly." See the New Cambridge edition, pp. 275–76, for an explanation of the F omissions in this scene.

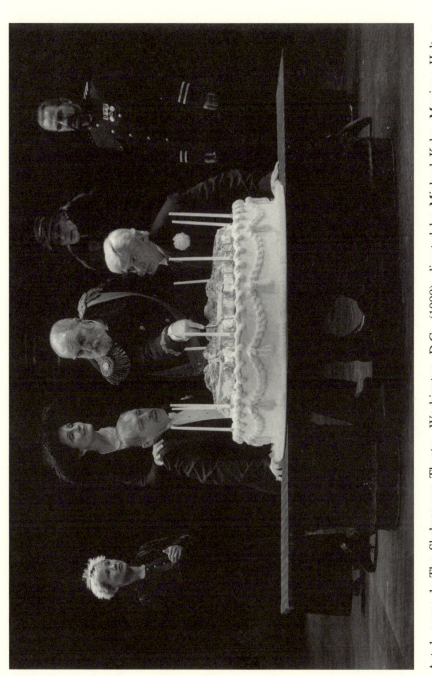

Act 1, scene 1: The Shakespeare Theatre, Washington, D.C., (1999), directed by Michael Kahn. Monique Holt as Cordelia, Jennifer Harmon as Regan, Ralph Cosham as Cornwall, Ten van Griethuysen as Lear, William Whitehead as Albany, Tana Hicken as Gonerill, Harry Wronowicz as Kent (1999). Photo by Carol Rosegg. Used with permission.

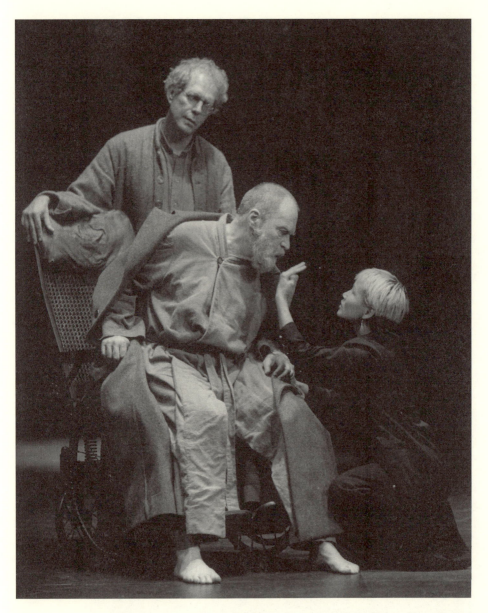

Act 1, scene 1: The Shakespeare Theatre, Washington, D.C. (1999), directed by Michael Kahn. Floyd King as the Fool, Ted van Griethuysen as Lear, Monique Holt as Cordelia (1999). Photo by Carol Rosegg. Used with permission.

Act 2, scene 4: Kent in the stocks, illustrated by Gordon Browne in *The Complete Works of William Shakespeare*, ed. Henry Irving and Frank A. Moorehead (London, 1899).

Act 3, scene 7: The Professional Theatre Training Program, University of Delaware, directed by Jewel Walker (1990). Ira Rosenberg as Gloucester, Elizabeth Heflin as Regan. Photo by William Browning. Used with permission.

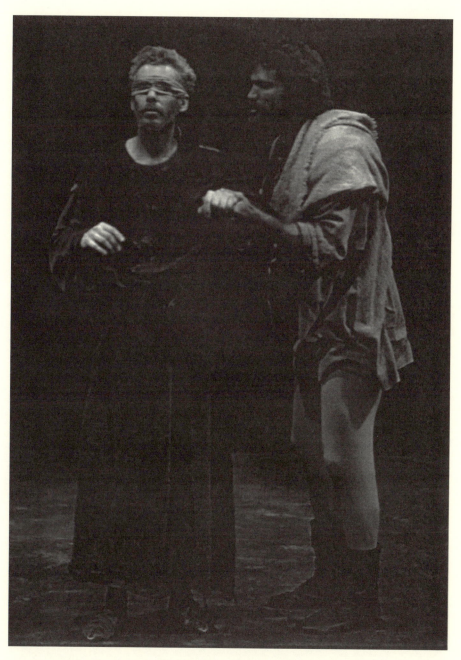

Act 4, scene 1: The Professional Theatre Training Program, University of Delaware (1990), directed by Jewel Walker (1990). Ira Rosenberg as Gloucester, Dennis Ryan as Edgar. Photo by William Browning. Used with permission.

Act 4, scene 5: Lear meets Gloucester and Edgar, illustrated by Gordon Browne in *The Complete Works of William Shakespeare*, ed. Henry Irving and Frank A. Moorehead (London, 1899).

Act 4, scene 5: The Shakespeare Theatre, Washington, D.C. (1999), directed by Michael Kahn. Ted van Griethuysen as Lear, David Sabin as Gloucester. Photo by Carol Rosegg. Used with permission.

Act 5, scene 3: The Shakespeare Theatre, Washington, D.C. (1999), directed by Michael Kahn. Ted van Griethuysen as Lear, Monique Holt as Cordelia (1999). Photo by Carol Rosegg. Used with permission.

5

CRITICAL APPROACHES

Besides the approaches taken in the foregoing chapters to analyzing and interpeting *King Lear*, other critical methodologies are available. Among them are: psychoanalytical criticism; feminist (or gender) criticism; linguistic analysis; myth, ritual, and folklore studies; Christian interpretations; and analysis through the New Historicism and Cultural Materialism. Some of these approaches overlap with those used earlier, and some overlap among themselves, inevitably, as no single critical methodology is or can be entirely divorced from others. Each makes its own contribution to the interpretation of *King Lear*, however, and collectively they provide a more comprehensive understanding of this great play.

PSYCHOANALYTICAL CRITICISM

Psychoanalytical criticism of *King Lear* begins with Sigmund Freud's essay, "The Theme of the Three Caskets,"[1] which discusses not only the casket story in Shakespeare's *The Merchant of Venice*, but also the three daughters in *King Lear* and their significance in both mythical and psychological terms. In fact, Freud was more interested in *King Lear* than in Shakespeare's earlier play. He saw in Lear's three daughters a representation of the three fates of Greek myth, the Morai, the third goddess being Atropos, the Goddess of Death. In rejecting Cordelia, Lear rejects Death. For Cordelia's reticence, her reluctance to speak ("What shall Cordelia speak? Love, and be silent," 1.1.57) is associated with dumbness, which, in dreams, psychoanalysts interpret as a representation of death.[2] Freud's interpretation of the final scene is illuminating:

Cordelia is death. . . . She is the Death-goddess who, like the Valkyrie in German mythology, carries away the dead hero from the battlefield. Eternal wisdom, clothed in primaeval myth, bids the old man renounce love, choose death and make friends with the necessity of dying. (p. 301)

In "The Avoidance of Love: A Reading of *King Lear*,"[3] Stanley Cavell approaches the psychological implications of Lear's action somewhat differently. He argues that Lear does not really want love but tries to avoid it; hence, he encourages and rewards flattery instead. Cavell says, furthermore, that Cordelia "threatens to expose both his plan for returning false love with no love, and expose the necessity for that plan— [Lear's] terror of being loved, of needing love" (p. 62). Complicating Lear's problem, or underlying it, is his inability to recognize himself and hence his desire to avoid being recognized, a problem Gloucester also has (pp. 45–46). As Regan says of her father at the end of the first scene, "he hath ever but slenderly known himself" (1.1.284–85).[4]

Why does Lear avoid love? Why does he wish not to be recognized? Cavell's hypothesis is that Lear fears exposure, self-revelation. What powerfully motivates Lear's behavior in the first scene is his sense of shame (pp. 57–59). Believing he does not deserve love or cannot return love, he bribes his daughters to offer him false love in exchange for a third of his kingdom. But Cordelia can only offer him true love, which enkindles his wrath, since it risks self-exposure. As Cavell says, "For some spirits, to be loved knowing you cannot return that love is the most radical of psychic tortures" (p. 61), and it eventually drives Lear insane.[5]

Cavell also analyzes Gloucester's plight in the parallel plot. Like Lear, Gloucester is motivated by shame, as the opening dialogue with Kent demonstrates. But he is ashamed of the wrong thing. It is not begetting Edmond that he should be most ashamed of, according to Cavell, but his refusal to acknowledge "*him* as a son or a person, with *his* feelings of illegitimacy and being cast out" (p. 48). This failure to recognize Edmond properly is a failure, too, and more significantly, "to let others recognize you, a fear of what is revealed to them, an avoidance of their eyes" (p. 49). Gloucester therefore suffers the punishment he inflicts:

In his respectability, he avoided eyes; when respectability falls away and the disreputable come to power, his eyes are avoided. In the fear of Gloucester's poor eyes there is the promise that cruelty can be overcome, and instruction about how it can be overcome. That is the content which justifies the scene of his blinding, aesthetically, psychologically, morally. (pp. 49–50)

Cavell then proceeds to show further linkages between the two plots and asks why is it that Gloucester is the one whose recognition Lear is first able to bear? The obvious answer is, of course, that Gloucester is blind; thus, Lear can be recognized without being seen, "without having to bear eyes upon himself" (p. 50). When he is sure that Gloucester cannot see, Lear recognizes him (4.5.168–69). But he runs away when Cordelia's men come to rescue him, not because he is mad and cannot distinguish friends from enemies, but because he knows that recognition of himself is imminent, and madness will not rescue him from that recognition (p. 52).

Cavell further considers another linkage between the two plots, asking what Lear is confronted by in acknowledging Gloucester. He answers that Gloucester has now become Lear's double, and what comes to the surface in their meeting is Lear's submerged mind. It is this, Cavell asserts, that gives the scene its particular terror. "In this fusion of plots and identities, we have the great image, the double or mirror image, of everyman who has gone to every length to avoid himself, caught at the moment of coming upon himself face to face" (p. 52).[6]

Finally, Cavell asks the important question, Why does Cordelia die? He replies that it is best answered not by asking what is the meaning of her death, but by asking what killed her. He begins by analyzing Lear's reaction to their going to prison, which he regards as a repetition of Lear's strategy in 1.1, or "a new tactic designed to win the old game" (p. 68). When Cordelia asks if they will see Regan and Gonerill, Lear emphatically rejects the suggestion. Now that his love is revealed, he wants it to be confined, out of sight. "He has come to accept his love, not by making room in the world for it, but by denying its relevance to the world" (p. 69). Hence, he flees from the world by going to prison with Cordelia. As "God's spies," he and Cordelia will look upon others but not be seen by them. In everything now, Cavell says, Lear is "not experiencing reconciliation with a daughter, but a partnership in a mystic marriage" (ibid.). In speaking of their "sacrifice" (5.3.20), Lear connects love and death in his mind, or death as payment for granting love: his own death, because acknowledging love means the annihilation of himself; her death, because he knows, as he knew from the beginning, that he is impotent to sustain her love (p. 70).

As they go off to prison, Lear sees Cordelia weeping. In his interpretation of these lines, Cavell answers the question of Cordelia's death:

> Lear imagines that [Cordelia] is crying for the reasons that he is on the verge of tears—the old reasons, the sense of impotence, shame, loss. But *her* reasons for tears do not occur to him, that she sees him as he is, as he was, that he is unable to take his last chance; that he, at the farthest edge of life, must again sacrifice her, again abdicate his responsibilities; and that he cannot know what he asks. And yet, seeing that, it is for him that she is cast down. Upon such knowledge the gods themselves throw incense. (p. 72)

When he carries Cordelia in his arms at the end, Lear says, "I might have saved her" (5.3.244). Indeed he might have, both at the beginning and at the end, had he done "what every love requires," Cavell says, "put himself aside long enough to see through to her, and be seen through" (p. 73). His need, however, or his interpretation of his need, has become her sentence.

Cavell does not dwell on the incest motif per se in *King Lear*, though it is a favorite among psychoanalytical critics. One of the first to offer an extended discussion of it is Arpad Pauncz, who developed what he refers to as the "Lear Complex."[7] He defines this as an attempt to account for the specific erotic attachment of the father for his daughter (p. 58). It is the reverse of the Oedipus complex, insofar as the fixation is not that of the child on the parent but the other way round (the debt to Freudian analysis is obvious). Pauncz says that the key to an understanding of Lear's tragedy is in the first scene: "Lear not only loves his daughters, he is also in love with them, especially with the youngest one" (p. 60). The division of his land is therefore not solely because of age and weariness, but a kind of "love-suit" for their favor; and when he is rejected, he reacts as "any temperamental, fiery, imperious suitor" would have done in those circumstances. Moreover, Lear's daughters know their father's true interests; they are—all except Cordelia—"willing, at least ostensibly, to submit to the wishes of the father" (pp. 61–62).[8]

Aware of her real duties and the impossibility of her father's demands, Cordelia does not submit; instead, she impugns both her sisters' adulation and the offers that she knows can never be fulfilled. As evidence of Lear's underlying motives, Pauncz says that, instead of getting rid of his hated child, he almost persuades her suitors from an alliance with her (p. 63). But the King of France, who is already emotionally involved, seems to sense the real meaning of the situation and carries Cordelia away. Her return is occasioned by her sisters' ingratitude, which itself is occasioned by their recognition of Cordelia's place in Lear's affections. But in Pauncz's interpretation Gonerill and Regan's ingratitude becomes a necessity for the working out of Lear's fate and his reunion with Cordelia. Even had the older daughters treated their father kindly, he could not have been happy with them, for his heart belonged to Cordelia (pp. 66–67).

Pauncz further supports his argument by noting Lear's obsession with sexuality in the storm scenes and later at Dover Beach. Copulation, incest, adultery are all explicitly mentioned in his sexual revulsion; erotic images seem to dominate his mental life (p. 70). Some of these images seem to Pauncz to be personally determined: Pauncz quotes 4.5.105–25 and later 4.5.152–55, which he sees as Lear's wanting a kind of self-vindication for his own lustfulness (p. 71). Pauncz also cites 4.5.178–79, Lear's expressed desire to kill his sons-in-law and concludes that "Lear does not become mad because he suffers from some complexes, but in the course of his madness all possible complexes become meaningful and obvious" (p. 77). The complexes, he adds significantly, do not make the man; but when Shakespeare lets the whole man become mad, new perspectives open up that enlighten areas of human experience.[9]

Many years later, Mark J. Blechner also considered the problem of incest in an article called "King Lear, King Leir, and Incest Wishes."[10] Like Pauncz, he focuses on the first scene and the many questions it raises concerning the love contest. He says that all the contradictions and unanswered questions suggest an unstated and, in today's psychoanalytical language, unconscious motivation (p. 312). In Lear's banishment of Cordelia, Blechner finds an unconscious wish, which becomes clearer by comparing Shakespeare's play to the source in *King Leir*. Noting important differences between the two plays—the motivations for and the circumstances in which the love contest takes place—Blechner believes that Shakespeare's Lear, who knows his youngest daughter will not engage in flattery, unconsciously hopes that Cordelia will say she loves him alone and reject all suitors for her hand in marriage. Lear may be carrying out "an unconscious plan to embarrass her in public, causing her to lose her dowry, and thereby preventing her from marrying" (p. 314).[11] After all, Lear in his old age faces the terrors of loneliness: his wife is dead, two daughters are already married (unlike the daughters in *King Leir*), and his youngest is almost about to be. "We have, then, the pathos of an old man, horribly alone, seeking, perhaps erotically but certainly passionately, to maintain the companionship and intimacy with his one daughter who remains unattached" (p. 315). The contest scene occasions the outbreak of that passion, making it both conscious and public.

Blechner adduces other evidence from the play and its comparison with the old *King Leir* to make his case. Perhaps the most important evidence is the ending, in which the King of France is entirely absent and Lear and Cordelia are reunited; "for only when Cordelia is separated from her husband is she fully available for Lear's love-making, which is the resolution of the play from the point of view of Lear's unconscious wish" (p. 318). In the final moments, having killed the slave who hanged Cordelia, and carrying her in his arms, Lear exhibits enormous strength, despite all he has endured. Blechner attributes this to "the power of a life's passion come forth" (p. 319) and compares Lear's last lines to the *Liebestod* (love-death) at the end of Wagner's *Tristan und Isolde*. He concludes that *King Lear* is a "love-tragedy" between father and daughter. In the final scene, the incest taboo is broken, Lear's love is expressed, "and, as in nearly all tragedies in which a taboo has been broken, the transgressing characters die" (ibid.).[12]

The parallel Gloucester plot also lends itself to psychoanalytical interpretation, as I have shown in an article on Gloucester's blinding.[13] For psychoanalytical critics, blinding, particularly tearing out of the eyes, symbolically represents castration.[14] An adulterer seen in these terms, Gloucester thus receives an appropriate punishment. Speaking of their father, Edgar says as much to his dying brother:

> The gods are just, and of our pleasant vices
> Make instruments to plague us.
> The dark and vicious place where thee he got
> Cost him his eyes.(5.3.160–63)

Historically, too, blinding as a punishment for sexual license was recognized. Elizabethans used mutilation of various kinds as punishment for crimes, but neither blinding nor castration is recorded as one of them, although the homily "Against Whoredom and Adultery" reminded parishioners of biblical punishments, and the Locrensians were specifically mentioned for blinding their malefactors.[15]

GENDER CRITICISM

Gender criticism, or what formerly was called feminist criticism, arose in the United States partly out of the civil rights movement of the 1950s and 1960s. Insofar as it is an attempt to understand the nature of woman and relationships between the sexes, it also stems directly or indirectly from some aspects of psychoanalytical criticism, with which it is closely associated. The practitioners of gender criticism are not usually psychoanalysts themselves, but many are well informed about various modes of psychoanalysis, whether or not they take a specifically designated psychoanalytical approach to their subject. Freud and his perceived bias against women is of course the bête noire of these critics, who have attempted to found a more evenhanded critique of sexuality and of gender relations.

Patriarchy is the other and older nemesis. Much of gender criticism is directed against patriarchal structures in literature as in life—against, that is, male domination of the female. Recent scholarship has shown, however, that in the early modern period—the period when Shakespeare wrote *King Lear*—the situation was more complicated than a simple, reductionist view of patriarchy makes it appear. Women had their own ways of challenging male authority, then as now.[16] The circumstances surrounding the case of Sir Brian Annesley and his daughters represent just one example testifying to this fact in real life, just as King Lear's daughters and other women in Elizabethan and Jacobean drama testify to it in literature.

In the introduction to one of the first anthologies of feminist criticism (as it was then known), *The Woman's Part* (1980), the editors begin by attempting to define their subject. Feminist criticism, they say, "pays acute attention to the woman's part in literature. But it is not only and not always feminocentric, for it examines both men and women and the social structures that shape them."[17] Two decades later, much of this agenda has been accomplished, though much remains, and gender studies—with or without a particular point of view—have become increasingly important. They have opened new avenues of research and understanding in Shakespeare studies that can be fruitful and rewarding.

Kate McLuskie's essay, "The Patriarchal Bard: Feminist Criticism and Shakespeare: *King Lear* and *Measure for Measure*,"[18] has become a classic among feminist approaches to *King Lear*, as well as a primary locus for feminist criticism in general. After a brief but succinct critique of earlier feminist criticism of Shakespeare, as in the work of Juliet Dusinberre, Linda Bamber, Marilyn French, Coppélia Kahn, and others, McLuskie analyzes *Measure for Measure* in feminist terms and then *King Lear*. As her title indicates, she sees the play as a defence of patriarchy, the major form of Renaissance political and domestic subju-

gation of women. If tragedy offers a view of universal human nature, as
some critics claim, the human nature implied in its moral and aesthetic
satisfactions, McLuskie argues, are most often explicitly male. "In *King
Lear* for example, the narrative and its dramatisation present a connection
between sexual insubordination and anarchy, and the connection is given
an explicitly misogynist emphasis" (p. 98).

McLuskie goes on to demonstrate her thesis by citing the presentation
of Gonerill and Regan. "Family relations in this play," she says, "are
seen as fixed and determined, and any movement within them is portrayed as a destructive reversal of rightful order (see I.iv)" (ibid.). The
elder daughters' treatment of their father is "a fundamental violation of
human nature." The resulting chaos at the end of the play, moreover, is
presented in gendered terms in which patriarchy emerges once again as
"the only form of social organization strong enough to hold chaos at
bay" (p. 99). Cordelia's role serves less as a redemption of womankind
than as an example of patriarchy restored. Earlier, her refusal to play the
game Lear has demanded of his daughters in 1.1 shows that a rupture
of the established order of obedience to the patriarch is tantamount to
the destruction of nature itself, as Lear maintains in his vocal outrage at
her behavior (see 1.1.103–20).

Coppélia Kahn's essay, "The Absent Mother in 'King Lear',"[19] depends more heavily than McLuskie's on psychoanalytical theory and
historical documents. Her emphasis is not so much on the misogyny of
patriarchy, though she acknowledges it, or on the incest motif, though
she acknowledges that as well. She focuses more fully instead on the
"imprint of mothering on the male psyche," as it is revealed in *King
Lear* (p. 94), and especially (as her title proclaims) the effect of the
mother's conspicuous absence in "a patriarchal conception of the family
in which children owe their existence to their fathers alone" (p. 95). She
sees family relationships and gender identity central to Shakespeare's
imagination, as they were to church and state in his period, and she
interprets crucial aspects of *King Lear* accordingly.

Like the psychoanalytical critics discussed above, Kahn begins her
analysis of the play by concentrating on the first scene. She sees there
that "the socially-ordained, developmentally appropriate surrender of
Cordelia as daughter–wife—the renunciation of her as incestuous object—awakens a deeper emotional need in Lear: the need for Cordelia
as daughter–mother" (p. 99). Like Stanley Cavell, Kahn recognizes
Lear's suppression of his need for love, which breaks out, however, in

ways that cause him both rage and anguish, as evidenced in part by *hysterica passio*, or "the mother"—his awareness of vulnerability and dependency—that Lear futilely tries to keep down. "In a striking series of images in which parent-child, father-daughter, and husband-wife relationships are reversed and confounded, Lear re-enacts a childlike rage against the absent or rejecting mother as figured in his daughters" (p. 100). By the end of the play, thanks to the ministering of Cordelia who has returned from France to succor him, Lear comes closer than ever before to "a mature acceptance of human dependency" (p. 107). When he awakens from the healing sleep in 4.6 and says, "For, as I am a man, I think this lady / To be my child Cordelia" (66–67), Lear not only acknowledges his manhood and his daughter's womanhood, but also Cordelia as his child, the relationship he had renounced in the first scene. Now, he is no longer threatened by her autonomy as a person and is intent on creating a new relationship with her based on this recognition. Citing 5.3.8–11, Kahn argues that parent and child are equal, "the gestures of deference that ordinarily denote patriarchal authority now transformed into signs of reciprocal love" (p. 108).

Cordelia's death, of course, prevents Lear from living out the fantasy that he imagines of their life together in prison. At the same time, it forces him to recognize once more that a daughter cannot be a mother, or that the only loving woman in his world is totally and irrevocally lost to him—a recognition that, in striving to revive her, perhaps he tries to reject. Shakespeare may have departed from his sources to let Cordelia die, Kahn says, because "he wanted to confront as starkly as possible the pain and separation from the mother" (p. 113), the theme Kahn pursues throughout her essay. At the end of the play, only men are left, and it remains for Shakespeare in his last plays, in the world of pastoral romance, to show how masculine authority can properly find mothers in its daughters, in Marina, Perdita, and Miranda.

Anticipating, in part, Kahn's essay, Lynda E. Boose relates the opening scene and its aftermath to the marriage ritual in "The Father of the Bride."[20] She begins by analyzing the church marriage service with specific reference to its underlying substructures of ritual. Citing the work of Arnold van Gennep, Boose notes that the marriage service contains the full pattern of the rites of passage: separation, transition, and reincorporation. "When considered by itself," she says, the marriage service is "basically a separation rite preceding the transitional phase of consummation and culminating in the incorporation of a new family unit" (p. 208). Or, in other words, what the church service is all about is the separation of the daughter from the father, who is the person that gives her away.

Boose goes into considerable detail analyzing the ritual of separation, transition, and reincorporation, noting in passing that the mother of the bride is a wholly excluded figure. "Only the father must act out, must dramatize his loss before the audience of the community. Within the ritual of circumscription, the father is compelled to give his daughter to a rival male" (p. 211). For him, therefore, the marriage ceremony represents an act of renunciation. In the crucial opening scene of *King Lear*, Lear must at last confront what he has apparently delayed up till now: the decision as to who will take Cordelia as his wife. But, as Boose remarks, and as others have also noted (see above), "instead of justly relinquishing his daughter, Lear tries to effect a substitution of paternal divestitures: he portions out his kingdom as his 'daughters' several dowers,' attaching to Cordelia's share a stipulation designed to thwart her separation. In substituting his public paternity for his private one, the inherently indivisible entity for the one that biologically must divide and recombine, Lear violates both his kingly role in the hierarchical universe and his domestic one in the family" (p. 213). As his language indicates— for example, by saying that Cordelia is "adopted to our hate" (1.1.197)— Lear's motives, consciously or otherwise, are to keep Cordelia from marrying and so from separating from him.

Lear's strategy almost works. It does where Burgundy is concerned,[21] but not France, who substitutes for the dowry Lear had promised a dowry of his own. Again the church service is echoed (1.1.245–46), when France takes for poorer as for richer the daughter that has forsaken all others. And "in a parody of the ring rite," Lear then takes the golden coronet and parts it between his two sons-in-law, "an act that both dramatizes the consequences of dividing his realm and demonstrates the anguish he feels at losing his daughter to a husband" (p. 216). When Cordelia leaves without her father's blessing, dowered instead with his curse, the ritual of separation is incomplete and her future blighted. Like Rosalind in *As You Like It*, she must return "to be reincorporated with her father before she can undergo the ritual severance that will enable her to progress" (p. 217). But in rewriting the traditional ending, as found in *King Leir*, for example, Shakespeare demonstrates "the tragic failure of the family unit to divide, recombine, and regenerate" (ibid.). As Boose notes, the play ends with the death of all the fathers and all the daughters.

With Kent recognizing that he has "a journey . . . shortly to go," the only ones left are the widower Albany and the as yet unmarried Edgar.

NEW HISTORICISM AND CULTURAL MATERIALISM

Because in some respects New Historicism and Cultural Materialism share similar approaches, it will be instructive to consider them together. In his chapter "Using History" in *William Shakespeare: "King Lear,"* Terence Hawkes discusses their similarities and contrasts both to the old historical approach, which tends to use history primarily as the background for works of literature. In so doing, the older historicism privileged literature. The New Historicism has attempted to forge a new relationship between history and literature, radically readjusting the balance so that literature does not enjoy its hitherto privileged position. Or, as Hawkes puts the case:

> On the one hand, it [the New Historicism] represents a reaction against an a-historical or 'idealist' view of the world in which an apparently free-floating and autonomous body of writing called 'literature' serves as the repository of the universal values of a supposedly permanent 'human nature'. On the other, it constitutes a rejection of the presuppositions of a 'history of ideas' which tends to regard literature as a static mirror of its time. Its 'newness' lies precisely in its determination to reposition 'literature' altogether, to perceive literary texts as active constituent *elements* and *aspects* of their time, participants in, not mirrors of it; respondent to and involved with numerous other enterprises, such as the law, marriage, religion, and government, all engaged in the production of 'texts' and, as a result, of the cultural meanings that finally constitute a way of life.[22]

A good example of a New Historical approach to *King Lear* is Stephen Greenblatt's essay, "Shakespeare and the Exorcists."[23] Greenblatt shows how Samuel Harsnett's tractate, *A Declaration of Egregious Popish Impostures* (1603) not only provided the source for much of Edgar's language as Tom o'Bedlam; it also provoked a more general response to Harsnett, who saw Catholic exorcism as a kind of theatrical enterprise. According to Greenblatt, the relation between Harsnett's book and Shakespeare's play "enables us to glimpse with unusual clarity and precision the institutional negotiation and exchange of social energy"

(p. 88). One aspect of this negotiation and exchange of social energy was the struggle to define the sacred, a definition that involved secular as well as religious institutions. In that struggle, Harsnett's *Declaration* was a weapon designed to support the established Church of England against competing religious authorities. It attempted to eliminate rivalrous, charismatic religious authority, specifically the charismatic authority of exorcism as practiced by Roman Catholic priests.

Greenblatt spends a good deal of his essay reviewing the hold that Catholic and even some Protestant exorcists had on English men and women in the sixteenth century. "As voluminous contemporary accounts declare . . . exorcisms were moving testimonials to the power of the true faith" (p. 90). Harsnett determined to expose the fraudulence of such exorcisms, to show that accounts of demonic possession were based upon illusion, not reality, which nevertheless made a powerful impression—as it was intended to do—in the minds of the audience. What seemed spontaneous, he argued, was "in fact carefully scripted, from the shaping of audience expectations to the rehearsal of the performers" (p. 93). To demystify exorcism definitively, therefore, Harsnett needed to demonstrate not only that the ritual was empty, but why it was so effective. He needed, in other words, to find "an explanatory model, at once metaphor and analytical tool" by which beholders could see fraud where once they saw God (p. 98). The model he seized upon was in theater, since he recognized that "Performance kills belief; or rather acknowledging theatricality kills the credibility of the supernatural" (p. 100).

What does all this have to do with Shakespeare and specifically *King Lear*? First of all, Harsnett did not attack the theater as such. He was not among those puritanical clergymen who found in the theater licentious entertainment that was to be avoided if not eradicated. On the contrary, Harsnett recognized theatrical illusion for what it was; he attacked exorcism as a form of theater that pretends it is not illusion but sober reality: "his polemic virtually depends upon the existence of an officially designated commercial theater, marked off openly from all other forms and ceremonies of public life precisely by virtue of its freely acknowledged fictionality" (p. 105). Shakespeare recognized this distinction and in earlier plays, like *The Comedy of Errors* (1590), he had played with the relationships of theater, illusion, and spurious possession. With such frank admissions of illusion, as voiced, for example, in Puck's epilogue in *A Midsummer Night's Dream*, Shakespeare could open the theater to Harsnett's polemic. "Indeed," Greenblatt says, "as if Harsnett's momentum carried *him* into the theater along with the fraud he hotly pursues, Shakespeare in *King Lear* stages not only exorcism, but Harsnett *on* exorcism," as examples of Edgar's mad discourse, which borrows many terms used in the *Declaration*, demonstrates (p. 106).

But Shakespeare found more than a source for Edgar's vocabulary in Harsnett. He also found the *inauthenticity* of the theatrical role. As in the scene at Dover Beach where Edgar persuades his father that he has jumped from a cliff, Shakespeare's theater elicits from us "complicity rather than belief. Demonic possession is responsibly marked out for the audience as a theatrical fraud" (p. 108). "*King Lear*'s relation to Harsnett's book is one of reiteration then, a reiteration that signals a deeper and unexpressed institutional exchange. The official church dismantles and cedes to the players the powerful mechanisms of an unwanted and dangerous charisma; in return the players confirm the charge that those mechanisms are theatrical and hence illusory" (p. 109). But Greenblatt does not stop there. He argues, furthermore, that Harsnett's arguments are alienated from themselves when they make their appearance on the Shakespearean stage. He proceeds to demonstrate that not only have certain rituals and beliefs been debunked, but more profound issues have also been brought into question. Greenblatt notes, as many other critics have done, that throughout the play invocations to the gods repeatedly and insistently prove of no avail. He concludes that "if false religion is theater, and if the difference between true and false religion is the presence of theater, what happens when this difference is enacted in the theater? What happens . . . is that the official position is *emptied out*, even as it is loyally confirmed" (p. 114).[24]

Like the New Historicism, Cultural Materialism declines to privilege literature, but its approach takes a somewhat different path. While both concern themselves with social and political issues and the role of drama in the public theaters, New Historicists tend to see Shakespeare's plays as reinforcing the dominant order, whereas Cultural Materialists tend to interrogate them "to the point of subversion."[25] Early in his book on the play, for example, Terence Hawkes considers audience reaction to Edmond's opening soliloquy in 1.2. He notes how Edmond's speech and the way he delivers it may "bond" us to him in "a kind of anarchic fellowship—pitting 'us' against the petty restrictions of 'them' " (p. 21). At the same time, the play's structure modifies that response, complicating it and turning the slightest taste for Edmond's "disarming vigour" into "the very factor that empowers his evil" (ibid.). But does it, in fact? Does warming to Edmond here amount to condoning him later? The speech, Hawkes contends, is a good example of the sort of moment in a play where a "cultural-materialist" account of it asks a number of questions. The main question becomes, given these complications and "taints," How should we respond?

Hawkes answers his question by rejecting any "once-for-all" resolution, to accept that such undecidable moments are characteristic of all texts. He argues that, in the speech at hand, while the logic (what is said) pulls us one way, its rhetoric (how it is said) pulls us another. "In short, the story's clear injunction to us to disapprove of illegitimacy turns out to be drastically at odds with the rhythm, the tone, the gestures, the alliterative and bodily momentum which builds up its overwhelming energy" in Edmond's lines (p. 22). The confusion, the moment of clear contradiction, results in a release of energy that is both frightening and exciting. As someone whom society has tried to silence and to marginalize (he has been "out nine years, and away he shall again," 1.1.27–28), Edmond speaks on behalf of all such persons. By doing so, he threatens to move from the periphery to the center, an act that lies at the heart of *King Lear* (ibid.)

Hawkes later shows how society in *King Lear* then becomes altogether "unhinged" (p. 47). Roles inherited from generation to generation suddenly cease to become available. From out of this displacement, occasioned in part by acts of enclosure[26] (to which Shakespeare alludes by his representation of Edgar as a masterless man, and by Lear's reference to the "poor naked wretches" that inhabit his kingdom), our modern world has emerged. The push for self-aggrandisement that characterizes Gonerill, Regan, and Edmond also contributes to the cataclysmic breakdown of the old order. Hawkes thus sees *King Lear* as a play centering on gigantic changes that result in widespread unemployment, which in turn "runs its jagged, dislocating course through this society, undermining everybody from pauper to monarch, like a major earthquake" (p. 48).[27]

As if intent on his own upheavals, Hawkes's final chapter, "Instead of a Masterpiece," questions *King Lear*'s position as a consummate work of literature. No historicist view, he maintains, can countenance "universalist" attributions to its permanence or "essentialist" claims to its "transcendence of time, location, and way of life" (p. 58). He doubts "whether any human enterprise can operate beyond the limitations of culture and history, factors which shape all human activity" (ibid.). To make his point, he reviews the stage history of *King Lear*, noting that for 150 years, beginning in the late seventeenth century, Nahum Tate's redaction, or some version of it, held the stage instead of Shakespeare's orginal.[28]

Moreover, the very issue of that "original" is compromised by the variant forms in which the text has come down to us,[29] and the by no means universal acclaim the play has enjoyed over the centuries, until our present age. He concludes, then, that "There is no 'original', essential, unchanging *King Lear*. There is no final play 'play itself' to which we can at last turn. . . . there is no 'ideal' *King Lear*" (p. 61). What we have, instead, is "a material object, or set of objects, on which we can and do operate in order to produce a range of 'meanings' in aspects of which our society from time to time chooses to invest. The shift of emphasis involved here is crucial: it moves our attention from a concern with sameness to a concern with difference" (ibid.). This is a Cultural Materialist view of the matter, concerned as it is, basically, with the ways that a play like *King Lear* is processed by a society. In our society, Hawkes says, we generate its meanings by our own historical context, and that includes the horrors revealed by World War II, especially the Holocaust; the decline of the British Empire and the emergence of the United States as a superpower replacing Britain; and the beginning of the Atomic Age and everything it implies, particularly the possibility of universal cataclysm (p. 63).

Cultural Materialism derives largely from earlier Marxist criticism, for which Terry Eagleton is one of the most prominent advocates among Shakespeareans. He treats *King Lear* briefly but succinctly in his book, *William Shakespeare*.[30] After an acute analysis of the use of language in 1.1, Eagleton moves to a discussion of other kinds of excess in the play. While it is natural for human beings to transcend their own limits, this creative tendency to exceed oneself is also the source of destructiveness, a paradox that *King Lear* explores (p. 88). This "difficult dialectic" poses the problem of respecting the norm while at the same time going beyond it. Excess may become too excessive, "yet such superfluity is also precisely that which marks off men and women from the inhuman precision of beasts, or indeed of Goneril and Regan" (ibid.).

Lear's daughters cannot understand why their father requires a retinue of a hundred knights, and they may have a point, Eagleton concedes. But they miss the more important point that Lear tries to explain in his speech beginning, "O reason not the need" (2.4.257 ff.). If there is no *reason* why human beings should delight in more than is strictly necessary for their survival, it is nonetheless "structural" to us, as human beings and not beasts, that demand should extend beyond minimal need. On the other hand, too many material possessions may inhibit one's ability to feel compassion, to sympathize with the misery of others. This insight comes to Lear out in the storm just before he comes face to face with Edgar as Poor Tom (3.4.33–36). It also comes to Gloucester after he is blinded (4.1.62–66), important passages that Eagleton quotes. Counterbalancing this destructive surplus or excess is Cordelia's forgiveness of her father, which goes well beyond the strict requirements of justice. As Eagleton says, "Cordelia blends largesse and limitation on her first appearance in the play, when she reminds Lear that her love, though freely given, must be properly divided between himself and her future husband" (p. 89). In so doing, she resolves in advance many of the play's formal antinomies; but in dying, she presents another problem that the play does not resolve, or as Eagleton concludes: "It is not, after all, simply a matter of reconciling fixed opposites: it is a matter of regulating what would seem an ineradicable contradiction in the material structure of the human creature. *King Lear* is a tragedy because it stares this contradiction full in the face, aware that no poetic symbolism is adequate to resolve it" (p. 90).

LINGUISTIC ANALYSIS

Shakespeare's plays are made of language, and the analysis of language has interested scholars and critics for a very long time. Under this heading, I include analysis of syntax, grammar, and diction, but also imagery, tropes, tone, and other aspects of language that lend themselves to objective analysis and the insights that may result.

Caroline Spurgeon's book on Shakespeare's imagery pioneered the study of image patterns and their significance.[31] Spurgeon was as much interested in what these images revealed about Shakespeare, man and poet, as she was in what they told us about his work, but here we need only be concerned with the imagery of *King Lear*, insofar as it provides yet another approach to understanding what happens in the play. Spurgeon was struck by "one overpowering and dominating continuous image," that of "a human body in anguished movement, tugged, wrenched, beaten, pierced, stung, scourged, dislocated, flayed, gashed, scalded, tortured and finally broken on the rack" (pp. 338–39). She cites several of the many verbs and images that appear in nearly every scene, both those dealing with Gloucester and those with Lear, that describe bodily movements usually involving pain. These verbs and images, moreover, are reinforced by words used in direct description, like those that describe the treatment of Gloucester in 3.7. The large number of animal images, such as tigers, kites, and serpents, augment the sensations of horror and bodily pain. Added to these are images of the elements in furious turmoil that appear, for instance, in the storm scenes in act 3, and that are described in terms of the human body by adjectives like "fretful" (3.1.4), "all-shaking" (3.2.6), and "roaring" (3.4.10).

The sense of bodily torture is unremitting, as in Gloucester's powerful image of wanton boys tearing apart flies (4.1.36) after he has had his eyes brutally torn out. Even as Lear awakens from the healing sleep in act 4, he imagines himself upon "a wheel of fire," his tears scalding him "like molten lead" (4.6.44–45). At the end, Kent pleads with Edgar not to try to revive the dying king, who has been stretched out long enough upon the "rack of this tough world" (5.3.287–89). By comparison with the imagery in *Othello*, written very near the time of *King Lear*, the torture in the latter is on "so vast and inhuman a scale, the cruelty of child to parent in the doubly repeated plot is so relentless and ferocious, that the jealous and petty malignity of Iago shrinks beside it," the difference in scale indicated as much, Spurgeon says, by the kinds of animal imagery used in the plays as by anything else (p. 336).

R. B. Heilman's book, *This Great Stage*, continues where Spurgeon left off, or rather develops in far more depth both a theory and its application as regards the imagery in *King Lear*.[32] He identifies and analyzes a number of patterns that Spurgeon overlooks and shows how pervasive and interrelated they are. These include the patterns of sight, smell, clothes, nature, madness, and values. Heilman argues that, as these patterns indicate, *King Lear* is finally "a play about the ways of looking at and assessing the world of human experience" (p. 28). He is also interested in the nature of the protagonist and tragic structure of the play, as these too are revealed through the image patterns, but here I shall concentrate mainly on one of the most important image patterns to demonstrate his critical method.

This is the imagery of sight, introduced early in the play, for example in the interchange between Lear and Kent, where Lear orders Kent out of his sight, and Kent urges the king to "See better . . . and let me still remain / The true blank of thine eye" (1.1.151–153).[33] But it is in the Gloucester plot that the image pattern becomes most pronounced. Gloucester has difficulty seeing clearly what Edmond is up to; in fact, when Edmond cleverly appears to hide the letter he has forged to implicate Edgar, Gloucester repeatedly says "Let's see" (1.2.34, 42) and argues, "if it be nothing, I shall not need spectacles" (1.2.34–35). But as

Heilman points out, spectacles are a symbol of what he does need (p. 45). Later, in act 2, when he enters with torches at night, the artificial illumination does him no good, as he falls deeper into Edmond's plot.

Gradually, Gloucester does begin to see, but too late. As he realizes what Lear's daughters are up to, he moves toward helping his old master, but errs again in confiding to Edmond. When he searches for Lear in the storm and carries a torch, this time the light is not ironic, Heilman says, but "symbolizes the first dim stage of enlightenment" (p. 47). The irony is that, just as Gloucester is beginning to take a stand, Edmond's plot against him matures, and he is taken prisoner in his own house by his enemies. Gonerill's threat, "Pluck out his eyes" (3.7.5), announces his fate, and he is deprived of those organs which had hitherto been of only superficial use to him. Once blinded, he learns the real truth concerning Edmond, but instead of dwelling on his evil son's treachery, he is concerned about his error in condemning Edgar: "O, my follies! Then Edgar was abused. / Kind gods, forgive me that, and prosper him" (3.7.90–91).

Gloucester now sees better than he has ever seen, but he still needs further insights, those that Edgar helps him to attain. "His physical and material loss," Heilman says, "is spiritual gain: he who would find his life must lose it" (p. 50). This is the basic paradox in *King Lear*, one of a series of paradoxes that, developed by the patterns of imagery, are the main structural determinants of the play. "To have eyes, and to see not, is to be at the mercy of evil, and thus to aid evil" (p. 51). If Gloucester is imposed upon by evil, Lear imposes it on himself, when he sets in motion the course of events that bring about his own and others' destruction. Lear progresses not, like Gloucester, from blind sight—"I stumbled when I saw" (4.1.19) to a seeing blindness—"I see it feelingly" (4.5.143); he moves from "an unwillingness to see, through a period of gradual anguished enlightenment, to a final passionate struggle to see" (p. 53). Heilman notes how much important action occurs during dark night (all of acts 2 and 3), reflecting Lear's fall gradually into mental darkness. But paradoxically again, Lear sees better when his normal faculties are gone, as in the Dover Beach scenes. As he awakens from madness, some of his first words are, appropriately, "Fair daylight?" (4.6.49), and he begins to recognize Cordelia, whom he once said he had never wanted to see again. "Of what she stands for, he will not lose sight again; yet in seeing her he will have to go through a final agony" (p. 57).

Madeleine Doran approaches the language of *King Lear* from a different direction in *Shakespeare's Dramatic Language*.[34] She begins by remarking how *King Lear* sounds very different from any of the other tragedies, presenting a world that is "archaic and remote—not only in time, but from the everyday naturalness and variety of discourse one hears in *Hamlet* or *Julius Caesar* or even *Antony and Cleopatra*" (p. 92). She attributes this difference in part to the fairy-tale aspect of the drama, in part to its "vague and featureless setting" (p. 93), but also to the style Shakespeare uses that distinguishes this play from the others. Taking note of Spurgeon's analysis of imagery, she argues that more is involved in the impressions we receive in *King Lear*, which she attributes to Shakespeare's use of imperatives, interrogatives, and assertions that abound in the play.

Citing Lear's opening speeches, Doran comments that "in no other Shakespearian tragedy do we hear so imperious a voice—so continually demanding, ordering, exclaiming, imprecating, demanding" (p. 94). Lear's typical syntax is that of command, the imperative mood ("Know," 1.1.32, "Tell me," 1.1.43, "Speak," 1.1.81), or some variant of it ("Let it be so," 1.1.102, "O let me not be mad," 1.5.37). But Lear also uses two forms of the indicative mood, the interrogative and the declarative sentence, for various purposes, both appropriately modulated. In his dialogue with Cordelia in 1.1, he uses all three modes of utterance, and as the play progresses, Doran says, "they will be varied and developed in complex harmonies and dissonances until they are brought to a resolution at the end" (p. 97).

Aware that style of syntax may be a function of character, Doran argues that Lear's voice is not the only one in which commands, assertions, and questions abound. She cites, for example, Kent's lines, 1.1.139–45, 158–60. Gonerill and Regan also use commands; so do Gloucester and, later, Edmond. Even Cordelia's prayer at 4.3.15–18, although different in tone, in syntax resembles Lear's commands, as does Gloucester's at 3.7.91. Similarities in the use of questions likewise emerge, especially in the Fool's speeches. In Doran's analysis, these elements of language are "an important means by which we enter (on a deeper level than formulated ideas) the peculiar universe of this play," for the world of a tragedy is created not only by what is said but by how it is said (p. 99). What determined Shakespeare's use of language peculiar to *King Lear*, Doran believes, was the basis of the tragedy in folktale, which uses much the same kind of linguistic structures.

In "Stylistic Design in *King Lear*," John Porter Houston also analyzes use of syntax in this play, but he is more interested in the kinds of sentence lengths and their syntactical constructions, especially the order of subject-verb-object, that distinguish various characters.[35] He notes the

use of inversion, as in Lear's speech at 1.1.58–62, to raise the tone of
his utterance, to invest somewhat ordinary words with greater distinc-
tiveness (p. 103). Houston also measures the lengths of sentences, particularly the frequency of short sentences in the imperative mood. Where
sentences are long and complicated, as in Gonerill's response to Lear at
1.1.50–56 and Regan's a few lines later, Gonerill's syntax is vague and
Regan's detail of expression somewhat obscure. But, Houston says, this
scarcely matters, since "the hazily synonymous phrases are supposed to
convey a love too great for grammatical or semantic precision" (p. 108).

Edmond's soliloquy at the beginning of 1.2 curiously appears in the
mold of a classical oration, although Edmond here is addressing only
himself. Houston distinguishes in it various aspects of Ciceronian ora-
tory. He comments perceptively that they may be used to convey the
element of artifice and craft in Edmond's character. His speech also
stands in contrast to the long sentences and speeches of the other male
characters besides Lear. Houston's analysis of Kent's narration of events
to Lear at 2.4.24–42 is a case in point. Although Kent gains employment
as Lear's servant Caius by affecting a blunt, plain manner, which he also
uses before Cornwall in 2.2, he here displays some virtuosity in language, partly to hasten the information Lear requires, but also to produce
what Houston calls "a jagged, colloquial syntactic effect, one perhaps
never actually found in speech but conveying belligerent neglect of
grammar" (p. 113). Kent's language does not follow predictable, rhetorical patterns, a trait that emphasizes his mysterious role in the background of the action.

Cordelia's language must have presented a special problem to Shakespeare. In 1.1 he had to give Cordelia lines that are distinctive from a
grammatical point of view, Houston says, but "scarcely beautiful by con-
ventional standards of the poetic or of the rhetorical finish" (p. 116).
Shakespeare devised a new style for Cordelia in act 4, heralded by the
the Gentleman's description of her return to England (in a scene following 4.2, unique to Q). Cordelia's opening lines in 4.3 evidence a new
lyric note in her very first long sentence. Her words show a penchant
now for imagery, symbolized by pastoral language and convention,
which associate her with the life of the countryside. "Thus, an important
but covert part of the sense of Cordelia's statement has been cast into
the grammatically subsidiary list of complements to *crown'd*" (p. 117).

Houston concludes by noting the wide variety of styles in the last two
acts of *King Lear*. The large number of scenes in act 4, he says, contributes to the effect of rapid succession and distinct changes in language

(p. 119). He calls attention to the grammatical styles, for example, of Albany and Gonerill in 4.2, but especially Gloucester's change of language after his blinding. Whereas, formerly, he tended more to prose than verse, he now uses striking imagery and syntactical inversions, as in 4.1.31–37. Much use is made also in the last two acts of plain but often pregnant statements, subtly rendered. And although Lear's language changes often in the last two acts, it tracks his psychological states, certainly if one compares his discourse in 4.5 with his language as he awakens in the next scene with Cordelia. There he attempts a more logical linking of clauses, as at 4.6.43–45 and 61–65, indicated by his use of connectives *but, that, yet, for,* and *nor.* It is as if he were learning rational speech again, Houston says (p. 121), although later in his euphoric mood (5.3.10–19), he resorts to polysyndeton, which suggests a lowering of logical and syntactical control, either from emotion or fatigue, or more likely a loss of ambient reality. Now it is as if Lear is trying, "by an almost incantatory stream of language, to envelop and isolate Cordelia and himself in a consoling private world" (p. 122). In no previous play has Shakespeare displayed so complex a stylistic design as in *King Lear,* Houston concludes, at least as far as blank verse is concerned (p. 123).

With this view, Frank Kermode seems to concur, although his analysis of the language of *King Lear* is far less technical than Houston's or even Doran's.[36] He is much more interested in the overall effect of the language of the play, particularly the effect of suffering that derives from the unsparing cruelty conveyed and the hopelessness of patience. He cites not only the blinding of Gloucester and its aftermath, but the scenes in the storm and those in acts 4 and 5. Of the meeting between Lear and Gloucester on Dover Beach, Kermode says: "The dreadful emphasis on blindness is the prime mark of Lear's madness and the play's cruelty, but nothing could be more sanely calculated than this dialogue" (p. 196). *King Lear* is "the craftiest as well as the most tremendous of Shakespeare's tragedies" (p. 200).

MYTH AND ARCHETYPAL CRITICISM

One of the earliest advocates and practitioners of myth and archetypal criticism was Maud Bodkin, whose *Archetypal Patterns in Poetry: Psychological Studies of the Imagination* (1934) drew upon the theories of Carl Jung and Gilbert Murray. She studied the way that certain themes, especially in tragedy, showed a persistence with the life of a community or race and compared the different forms they assumed. More recently, Northrop Frye developed the approach in "Archetypal Criticism: Theory of Myths," the third chapter of his monumental work, *Anatomy of Criticism* (1957). He begins his study of archetypes with the world of myth, which he defines as "an abstract or purely literary world of fictional and thematic design, unaffected by canons of plausible adaptation to familiar experience." The meaning or pattern of poetry is "a structure of imagery with conceptional implications."[37] This type of criticism has clear links to the analysis of image pattern discussed above, but extends well beyond it.

Frye distinguishes four basic patterns of myth in literature and relates them to the four seasons: spring (comedy), summer (romance), autumn (tragedy), winter (irony and satire). Here we need only concern ourselves with tragedy, or the mythos of autumn, in which Frye perceives "a mimesis of sacrifice" (p. 214):

> Tragedy is a paradoxical combination of a fearful sense of rightness (the hero must fall) and a pitying sense of wrongness (it is too bad that he falls). There is a similar paradox in the two elements of sacrifice. One of these is communion, the dividing of a heroic or divine body among a group which brings them into unity with, and as, that body. The other is propitiation, the sense that in spite of the communion the body really belongs to another, a greater, and a potentially wrathful power. (Ibid.)

The implications of these comments for *King Lear*, which Frye elsewhere invokes directly, are clear. So is his further comment, which relates to the play's ending: "As a mimesis of ritual, the tragic hero is not really killed or eaten, but the corresponding thing in art still takes place, a vision of death which draws the survivors into a new unity" (p. 215).

In his book on tragedy, Frye discusses *King Lear* and other Shakespearean tragedies together with Greek tragedy. At the end, he draws attention to the central myth of Christianity and the question whether tragedy is compatible with a Christian view of life.[38] While institutional Christianity is incompatible with the tragic vision, he says, the reality—the myth—of Christianity is very different. "The heroic effort which Christ made against the irony of universal death was, Christianity tells us, successful. But the earthly end of his career, so far as we can see it, was exactly the same as the end of a failure" (p. 117). Frye regards the religious example as an analogy to the tragic structure in Shakespeare.

In the "tragedy of isolation," the type that includes *King Lear*, "the hero becomes a scapegoat, a person excluded from his society and thereby left to face the full weight of absurdity and anguish that isolated man feels in nature" (p. 118). This is Lear's situation at the end of the play, with Cordelia dead, "never, never to come back to him" (p. 115).

In "The Artist Exploring the Primitive: *King Lear*,"[39] F. D. Hoeniger considers the origins of the Lear story both in the form that Shakespeare found it in prehistory and in the form in which he cast it ("highly unreal, utterly remote from any familiar history," p. 75). The play's hold upon us derives from Shakespeare's probing the depths of primal human experience far more than the original story did, especially in Lear's descent into the primitive world of chaos that his own disordered mind reveals as well as the chaos surrounding him. In Edgar's impersonation of the mad beggar, Tom o'Bedlam, as in the actions of Gonerill, Regan, Cornwall, and Edmond, Shakespeare further explores the primitive aspects of human nature. In his superstitiousness, Gloucester also reflects aspects of the primitive, although the worship of power and the lust after it, evidenced in the behavior of Lear, his villainous daughters, and Edmond, is a deeper and more disturbing primitive impulse.

Referring to the researches of the Italian ethnologist Giuseppe Cocchiara, Hoeniger demonstrates how *King Lear* adapts many elements of folktales.[40] Prominent among the folktales that show affinity with *King Lear* are those that center upon the theme of "love like salt," which Cocchiara, like other ethnologists, record.[41] They involve a love contest among a king's three daughters and the final reconciliation between the king and his banished daughter. The version from Corsica that Cocchiara cites includes the king's madness (not found in any of the Lear stories) and the heroine's care to restore him to sanity. This version also includes part of the Cinderella story, which other scholars also relate to the opening scene of *King Lear*.[42] Another element not found in the acknowledged sources that this story shares with *King Lear* is the motif of the disguise assumed by the banished person, although here it is the Cordelia figure that is disguised. Cocchiara also traces the folktales back to initiation rites among primitive peoples, a road Hoeniger is reluctant to travel with him, noting, nevertheless, some resemblances between Edgar's experience as Tom o'Bedlam and those very rites. The point Hoeniger establishes from all of this material and his own response to *King Lear* is that "Shakespeare's imagination, dwelling on the significance of the Lear story and reshaping it into a play of profound dramatic impact, recaptured elements from the primitive past that at some time were a fundamental part of its shape and meaning. Of course he not only re-captured, he transformed as well, to make of primitive horror and bru-tality the highest kind of art" (p. 86).

Maynard Mack refers to another archetype that likely influenced the shaping of *King Lear*, the Abasement of the Proud King.[43] In these sto-ries, a king is stripped of his power and made to serve variously as a court fool or madman and is tormented or mocked by others until he acknowledges his true position as a man among men, repents his former arrogance, and is restored to power. As in *King Lear*, there is humbling of pride, nakedness, cold, loss of identity, and madness. In one version, an angel takes the king's place and the king's repentance comes when, in a moment of insight, he notices a resemblance between himself and the great ruler Nebuchadnezzar, who was also brought low and lived many years merely on roots and grass. The king thus is moved to repent, and in his prayer he acknowledges himself to be "thy fool, Lord," whereas formerly he had always regarded himself as lord.

CHRISTIAN INTERPRETATIONS

Critics have been fond of seeing a morality structure in *King Lear* resembling an older form of drama still popular in Shakespeare's boy-hood.[44] Others have gone further and allegorized the structure of *King Lear*, seeing in Cordelia a Christ figure redeeming humanity, represented by King Lear. Clearly, as in Shakespeare's other plays, many biblical allusions and echoes appear; but it is one thing to notice them and rec-ognize the analogies, another to make a biblical narrative out of them. Most critics now agree that *King Lear* is not a "Christian" tragedy, partly for some of the reasons Northrop Frye developed in *Fools of Time* (pp. 116–17), but mainly because of the arguments William R. Elton has put forward in *"King Lear" and the Gods*.[45] As Elton says, Cordelia is far from being an emblem or image of Christ; she represents instead the pagan *prisca theologica*, or "virtuous heathen" view grounded in pre-Christian thought, which in some ways foreshadows Christian concepts of virtue, as may be seen also in Sir Philip Sidney's *Arcadia* and Sir Thomas More's *Utopia*.[46]

How then do biblical allusions function in Shakespeare's play? Though the setting is pre-Christian, the play was written and performed for a Christian audience—an audience, unlike today's, that could and did recognize the allusions and notice the analogies, for example, in

Cordelia's lines, "O dear father, / It is thy business that I go about" (4.3.23–24).[47] The play ends with a clear reference to Doomsday, but *King Lear* does not recapitulate the Book of Revelation.[48] Why then does Shakespeare introduce such references? To provide a wider dimension for the play's action. As Rosalie Colie says, "The use of biblical echo to suggest a morality past ordinary hopes allows us to work through the complicated paradoxes of the play to accept the essential, inevitable, unalterable limitations of human life."[49]

Although he does not allegorize the play, Roy Battenhouse's treatment in *Shakespearean Tragedy: Its Art and Christian Premises*[50] is one of the most thoroughgoing treatments of *King Lear* from a Christian perspective. He not only points out the many allusions and analogies to biblical incidents and scriptual writing, he also shows how the play, in his view, offers a Christian interpretation of events in a non-Christian setting. He says, for example, that Edmond's deathbed confession of his guilt and his impulse to do some good despite his own nature are prompted by Edgar's willingness to exchange charity with the brother he has just defeated in a duel (pp. 273–74). Similarly, Gloucester comes to recognize "The bounty and benison of heaven" (4.5.216) in his unknown guide, the disguised Edgar, who has helped him emerge from despair and who, moments later, will rescue him from Oswald's murderous intention. Divine providence is operative also in Albany's recognition of Gonerill's fate as "This judgement of the heavens" (5.3.205). Her downfall, moreover, is related to earlier strokes of justice, in Battenhouse's view, such as Edgar's intercepting of her letter and his victory over Edmond.

Lear acts in ignorance in 1.1, but as Battenhouse argues, his ignorance is "wilful ignorance"; Lear knows, or should know, better. "This point accords with St. Paul's explanation, in Romans 1, of how the Gentiles are culpable for their own tragedy: they have ignored a knowledge they partly had and could have had more fully" (p. 281). Cordelia fails the love test in 1.1, both from Lear's point of view and from a Christian one, too; but she later learns a "shepherding love" when she returns from France to care for her homeless, sick, and abused father (p. 283). Perhaps her change of heart owes something to the King of France's behavior, Battenhouse suggests. His rescuing love in 1.1 accords with "a new kind of law, which does not measure by merit, or by favors received, or by any customary bond of obligation" (p. 284); in other words, it accords with the Christian concept of love. France takes Cordelia for his bride "that he may perfect her—a concept that is basic to the New Testament idea of marriage" (p. 285). His act is thus "figurally" Christian, in contrast to the despairing naturalism of Gloucester.

Lear progresses to redemption through the purgatorial experience he endures, that is, through his gradual learning to put off an initial self-centeredness, as his divestment of clothing from act 3 onwards signifies. Battenhouse traces Lear from his early wish to divest himself of "cares of state" (which masks a covetous desire really for his own adulation), to relinquishment of his hopes for courtly pomp (but in a spirit of bitter savagery), finally to "a genuine and gentle humility, contaminated no longer by self-will" (p. 291). His awakening to Cordelia in 4.6 seems to Lear like a resurrection from the dead. Cordelia's tent becomes a kind of holy place, which, to Shakespeare's Christian audience, would recall the tabernacle of Old Testament times, where the Israelites celebrated deliverance from the Egyptians (p. 292). In the final scene, Lear's bending over the body of Cordelia would have reminded that audience, too, of the Deposition from the Cross, depicted in so many medieval paintings, a kind of inverted pietá.

"In order to be convincing, a Christian reading of *King Lear* must bravely push on," René Fortin says, "beyond the 'redemption' scenes of Act IV and take in fully the devastatingly ironic death of Cordelia."[51] Indeed it must, and Fortin attempts to do just this in his ensuing analysis. He recognizes with secular critics that the gods fail to provide the "chance which does redeem all sorrows" (5.3.240), the miracle of Cordelia's return to life. But he does not accept this as an indictment of Christian interpretation any more than it is an indictment of Christian belief, since mainstream Christianity does not presume God will intervene on call of his faithful (Fortin cites the relevant Christian authorities to support this view, p. 131). What Lear and Cordelia endure does not contradict the image of God that both Protestant and Catholic orthodoxy uphold. Fortin compares the action of the play, particularly as it concerns Lear's progress to deeper sight and insight, with parallel passages in the Book of Revelation, and then comes to the problem of Cordelia's death.

Because he believes secular critics isolate the scene of Cordelia's death, Fortin insists on placing it in the full context of the play. He notes its recapitulatory function: Lear is once again in the situation of the first scene, calling upon Cordelia to speak words of love and comfort to him, and getting a similar, silent response, or rather "Nothing." But Fortin explains this as "no more a denial of value than was her earlier silence" (p. 133). He goes on to argue that the apparent absence of redeeming goodness is no guarantee that it does not exist (p. 134). Though the world offers no "cheap consolations," we need not infer that God has forsaken the world (ibid.). The biblical echoes in *King Lear* may be an attempt to "demythologize" Christianity, to reassert the hiddenness of God against the "presumptuous pieties" and "shallow rationalism" that characters like Edgar and Albany express.

The death of Cordelia, in this view, supports rather than contradicts Revelation and the God of the New Testament, "being a God of faith seen but through a glass darkly" (p. 135). But Fortin is quick to maintain that such a Christian reading is not the definitive reading of *King Lear*. It neither invalidates secular readings nor supersedes them. But in admitting that both secular and religious interpretations may be valid, Fortin does not argue for critical relativism. Instead, his approach suggests something very similar to the "complementarity" that Norman Rabkin identifies in his study of Shakespeare, that is, Shakespeare's ability to present opposing but complementary views of an issue.[52] *King Lear* dramatizes the human quest for justice. It shows both our folly, callousness, and brutality *and* the perdurance of virtue under the most trying circumstances, along with a moral awakening under the pressures of adversity. "Calculations about what all this adds up to may differ, and differ markedly," Fortin concludes, "but it is most probably true that any interpretation of the play which denies that these are central concerns is simply wrong. The open form of tragedy, its respect for the limits of human experience, allows readers to draw different conclusions: enough is given to allow interpreters to 'see feelingly,' to infer an interpretation based upon their own personal experience of the play; but enough is withheld to compel respect for the tragic mystery" (p. 136).

NOTES

1. In *The Standard Edition of the Complete Psychological Works of Sigmund Freud*, trans. James Strachey (London: Hogarth Press, 1958), 291–301.

2. Ibid., pp. 295–96. Freud uses examples from several folktales to illustrate this point.

3. Cavell's essay originally appeared in *Must We Mean What We Say?* (1969), and is reprinted in *Disowning Knowledge in Six Plays of Shakespeare* (Cambridge: Cambridge University Press, 1987). The quotation is from the reprint, p. 62. All subsequent references are also from the reprint.

4. On the theme of self-knowledge, a prominent one in the Renaissance, see Paul A. Jorgenson, *Lear's Self-Discovery* (Berkeley and Los Angeles: University

of California Press, 1967), and Rolf Soellner, *Shakespeare's Patterns of Self-Knowledge* (Columbus: Ohio State University Press, 1972). Neither work, however, uses a particularly psychoanalytical approach.

5. Note Kent's explanation for Lear's refusal to see Cordelia at first when she returns from France to aid him: "A sovereign shame so elbows him." The passage appears only in Q, in the scene from act 4 that F omits: see the New Cambridge edition, p. 305, line 40.

6. Shortly afterwards, Cavell also considers why Edgar does not reveal himself to Gloucester sooner than he does, that he too avoids recognition, though for different reasons (pp. 54–57).

7. Arpad Pauncz, "Psychopathology of Shakespeare's 'King Lear'," *American Imago* 9 (1952), 57–78. Pauncz was anticipated in his analysis of the incest theme by J.S.H. Bransom in *The Tragedy of King Lear* (Oxford: Basil Blackwell, 1934), pp. 217–24.

8. Compare Jane Smiley's novel, *A Thousand Acres*, her adaptation of Shakespeare's play, in which incest is made explicit, when it is revealed that the Lear character has abused his daughters as children.

9. In a subsequent study, "The Lear Complex in World Literature," *American Imago* 11 (1954), 51–83, Pauncz extends his analysis of the Lear complex to other works of literature, including such diverse ones as Honoré de Balzac's *Pere Goriot*, Henry James's *Washington Square*, and George Eliot's *Silas Marner*. Indeed, the Lear complex, as Pauncz defines it, seems almost ubiquitous in world literature.

10. In *American Imago* 45 (1988), 309–25.

11. Compare Pauncz's hypothesis, noted above, that by his action Lear hopes to dissuade Cordelia's suitors from marrying her.

12. In a long endnote (n. 10, p. 324), Blechner continues his discussion of the taboo and its consequences. When taboo desires are renounced or resolved, he says, history or romance results, as in *King Leir*. When they are not, a tragic ending is inevitable, as in *King Lear*. He compares Shakespeare's *The Tempest* in this context, noting that the storm there, as in *King Lear*, symbolizes "the churning up of old impulses." But, in *The Tempest*, "Prospero ambivalently resigns himself to his age, yields his daughter in marriage, and ultimately bids farewell to his magical powers."

13. Jay L. Halio, "Gloucester's Blinding," *Shakespeare Quarterly* 43 (1992), 221–23.

14. In discussing the castration complex, Freud says that "the blinding with which Oedipus punishes himself after the discovery of his crime is, by the evidence of dreams, a symbolic substitute for castration" (*An Outline of Psycho-Analysis*, in *The Standard Edition*, ed. Strachey, vol. 23, p. 190).

15. See *Certain Sermons or Homilies (1547)*, ed. Ronald B. Bond (Toronto: University of Toronto Press, 1987), p. 183. For further psychoanalytical interpretations of *King Lear*, see Norman N. Holland, *Psychoanalysis and Shake-*

speare (New York: McGraw-Hill, 1966), pp. 214–19, and the collection of psychoanalytical essays in *Representing Shakespeare*, ed. Murray M. Schwartz and Coppélia Kahn (Baltimore: John Hopkins University Press, 1980). Although none of the essays in the latter is exclusively devoted to *King Lear*, many of them, such as David Willbern's "Shakespeare's Nothing," treat the play at least in part.

16. See Juliet Dusinberre, *Shakespeare and the Nature of Women*, 2nd ed. (New York: St. Martin's Press, 1996), p. xvii. Dusinberre's preface to the second edition, published twenty years after the first, surveys the development of gender criticism, especially but not exclusively related to Shakespeare studies.

17. *The Woman's Part: Feminist Criticism of Shakespeare*, ed. Carolyn Ruth Swift Lenz, Gayle Greene, and Carol Thomas Neely (Urbana: University of Illinois Press, 1980), p. 3.

18. In *Political Shakespeare*, ed. Jonathan Dollimore and Alan Sinfield (Ithaca: Cornell University Press, 1985), pp. 88–108.

19. In *Rewriting the Renaissance*, ed. Margaret Ferguson, Maureen Quilligan, and Nancy Vickers (Chicago: University of Chicago Press, 1986), pp. 33–49; reprinted in *New Casebooks: "King Lear,"* ed. Kiernan Ryan (New York: St. Martin's Press, 1992), pp. 92–113. References are to the reprint.

20. In *PMLA* 97 (1982), 325–47; adapted and reprinted in *Shakespeare's Middle Tragedies*, ed. David Young (Englewood Cliffs, N.J.: Prentice Hall, 1993), 207–20. References are to the reprint.

21. Boose notes how Lear, parodying the church service, mimes the priest at 1.1.196–99.

22. Terence Hawkes, *William Shakespeare: "King Lear"* (Plymouth, England: Northcote House, 1995), p. 11.

23. In Stephen Greenblatt, *Shakespearean Negotiations* (Berkeley: University of California Press, 1988), pp. 94–128; reprinted in *Critical Essays on Shakespeare's "King Lear,"* ed. Jay L. Halio (New York: G. K. Hall, 1996), pp. 88–121. References are to the reprint.

24. In an earlier version of this essay, printed in *Shakespeare and the Question of Theory*, ed. Patricia Parker and Geoffrey Hartman (1985), Greenblatt put the matter somewhat differently: "In Shakespeare, the realization that demonic possession is a theatrical imposture leads not to clarification—the clear-eyed satisfaction of the man who refuses to be gulled—but to a deeper uncertainty, a loss of moorings, in the face of evil" (p. 179).

25. Hawkes, p. 15, citing Jonathan Dollimore, "Critical Developments: Cultural Materialism, Feminism and Gender Critique, and New Historicism," in *Shakespeare: A Bibliographical Guide*, ed. Stanley Wells (Oxford: Oxford University Press, 1990), p. 414.

26. In his preceding chapter (p. 45), Hawkes refers to these enclosures, the means by which landowners consolidated their holdings by "enclosing" smaller

strips of land farmed by individual tenants into larger units worked by fewer laborers, resulting in growing unemployment and poverty among the populace.

27. Compare Kiernan Ryan, " 'King Lear': The Subversive Imagination," in *New Casebooks*, ed. Ryan, p. 78: "In *King Lear* the assault on traditional structures of social domination by a ruthlessly competitive and acquisitive individualism . . . is imaginatively refracted through the parallel generational conflicts which rip the families of Lear and Gloucester apart."

28. See the chapter on *King Lear* in performance below.

29. On this issue, see discussion of the textual history of *King Lear* in chapter 1, above.

30. Terry Eagleton, *William Shakespeare* (Oxford: Blackwell, 1986), pp. 76–83; reprinted in *New Casebooks*, ed. Ryan, pp. 84–91. References are to the reprint.

31. Caroline Spurgeon, *Shakespeare's Imagery and What It Tells Us* (Cambridge: Cambridge University Press, 1935).

32. Robert Bechtold Heilman, *This Great Stage: Image and Structure in* King Lear (Seattle: University of Washington Press, 1963; rpt. Greenwood Press, 1976). References are to the reprint.

33. For the gloss on "blank" as at once "target" and "pupil of the eye," see the New Cambridge edition, p. 104.

34. Madeleine Doran, *Shakespeare's Dramatic Language* (Madison: University of Wisconsin Press, 1976).

35. This is the title of Chapter 5 in Houston's *Shakespearean Sentences: A Study in Style and Syntax* (Baton Rouge: Louisiana State University Press, 1988), pp. 103–23.

36. Frank Kermode, *Shakespeare's Language* (New York: Farrar, Straus, Giroux, 2000), pp. 183–200.

37. Northrop Frye, *Anatomy of Criticism* (Princeton: Princeton University Press, 1957), p. 136.

38. Northrop Frye, *Fools of Time: Studies in Shakespearean Tragedy* (Toronto: University of Toronto Press, 1967), pp. 116–20.

39. In *Some Facets of "King Lear": Essays in Prismatic Criticism*, ed. Rosalie L. Colie and F. T. Flahiff (Toronto: University of Toronto Press, 1974), pp. 77–102; reprinted in *Critical Essays on Shakespeare's "King Lear,"* ed. Jay L. Halio (New York: G. K. Hall, 1996), pp. 75–87. References are to the reprint.

40. Giuseppe Cocchiara, *La Leggenda di re Lear (Studi di etnologia e folklore* 1) (Torino, 1932).

41. See, for example, Stith Thompson, *Motif-Index of Folk-Literature* (Bloomington: Indiana University Press, 1956), vol. 3, p. 432.

42. See Wilfrid Perrett, *The King Lear Story from Geoffrey of Monmouth to Shakespeare* (Berlin, 1904); Alan Dundes, " 'To love my father all': A Psychoanalytic Study of the Folktale Source of *King Lear*," in *Cinderella: A Casebook*, ed. Alan Dundes (1983), pp. 229–44; and compare Katherine Stockholder, "The

Multiple Genres of *King Lear*: Breaking the Archetypes," *Bucknell Review* 16 (1968), 45.

43. Maynard Mack, King Lear *in Our Time* (Berkeley: University of California Press, 1965), pp. 49–51. Mack cites a fuller discussion of the various forms of this story in Lillian H. Hornstein, *"King Robert of Sicily*: Analogues and Origins," *PMLA* 79 (1964), 13–21.

44. See Mack, pp. 56–66.

45. William R. Elton, *"King Lear" and the Gods*, 2nd ed. (Lexington: University Press of Kentucky, 1988). Originally published in 1966 by the Huntington Library.

46. Elton, pp. 38–42.

47. Compare Luke 2.49: "I must go about my fathers business?" (Geneva bible, 1582).

48. See Joseph Wittreich, *"Image of that Horror": History, Prophecy, and Apocalypse in "King Lear"* (San Marino, Calif.: Huntington Library, 1984).

49. Rosalie L. Colie, "The Energies of Endurance: Biblical Echo in *King Lear*," in *Some Facets*, p. 140. Compare Thomas P. Roche, Jr., " 'Nothing Almost Sees Miracles': Tragic Knowledge in *King Lear*," in *On* King Lear, ed. Lawrence Danson (Princeton: Princeton University Press, 1981), pp. 136–62. Roche maintains that *King Lear* introduces Christian imagery and motifs to suggest "the plight of man before the Christian era, that is, before the salvation of man by Christ's sacrifice was available" (p. 149).

50. Bloomington: Indiana University Press, 1969.

51. René Fortin, "Hermeneutical Circularity and Christian Interpretations of *King Lear*," in *Gaining upon Certainty: Selected Criticism* (Providence: Providence College Press, 1995), p. 130.

52. Norman Rabkin, *Shakespeare and the Common Understanding* (New York: Free Press, 1967).

6

THE PLAY IN PERFORMANCE

Echoing the view of the nineteenth-century critic, Charles Lamb, who believed *King Lear* was not actable, A. C. Bradley said, *"King Lear* is too huge for the stage."[1] Huge it certainly is, and it requires not only a great actor for the title role, but an excellent supporting cast, such as it is seldom possible to assemble for one production. Nevertheless, fine performances of the play have been enacted in recent years, as they have in the past, few and far between though they may have been.

Scarcely any records exist of the play's earliest performances. We may be sure that Richard Burbage, the leading actor of Shakespeare's company, the King's Men, played Lear. Many scholars believe that Robert Armin, who had replaced Will Kempe as the actor performing the fool's role in plays like *As You Like It* and *Twelfth Night*, must have played the Fool in *King Lear*. But William Ringler has argued very persuasively that Armin more likely played Edgar, since he was extremely good at playing multiple roles, such as the changes of character in parts he wrote for himself in his compositions for the stage; hence, Edgar's changes of character in *King Lear* would suit him very well. In Ringler's view, one of the boy actors played both the Fool and Cordelia. Given the relatively small number of professionals in the acting company (about fifteen; hired men, who played the parts of walk-ons, spear-carriers, and the like, were additional), doubling was not unusual, indeed often required, in performing Shakespearean and other Elizabethan plays. The Fool and Cordelia never appear together in any scene; in fact, after Cordelia departs in 1.1, the Fool does not appear until 1.4; and Cordelia does not reappear until the middle of act 4, long after the Fool is last seen in 3.6. This doubling, moreover, makes sense from a thematic viewpoint, since Cordelia and the Fool apparently have a close relationship. As the Knight says at 1.4.62–3, in reply to Lear's repeated asking for his Fool, whom he has not seen for some time, "Since my young lady's going into France, sir, the fool hath much pined away."[2]

From the title page of Q1, we know that *King Lear* was performed at court on St. Stephen's Day (December 26) in the Christmas holidays of 1606. The play, which had probably been first performed at the Globe, was an appropriate choice for the holiday season, for it was during this religious period (from Christmas until New Year's Day) that sermons emphasized humanity's folly and worldliness, and biblical readings on St. Stephen's Day exhorted parishioners to exercise patience in adversity and to offer hospitality to the poor and homeless.[3] How King James and his courtiers reacted to the performance we do not know, though certainly the theme of division of the kingdom must have struck a resounding chord in the sovereign and some of his ministers who had been trying to unify the realms of England and Scotland, a matter high on James's list of priorities when, as James VI of Scotland, he succeeded Elizabeth I to the throne of England.

No further record of performance for *King Lear* in London is extant during the Stuart period and not until after the restoration of the monarchy in 1660 do we again hear about its being played in London.[4] To judge from the revisions made on the Folio text, we may assume that the play was revived from time to time, most likely for performance at the Blackfriars Theatre after the King's Men started to perform there in 1609 as well as at the Globe. Puritans closed down all theaters in 1642, and they did not reopen for almost twenty years, when Charles II returned to his father's throne from his exile in France. French influence on the theater, as in many other respects, such as dress and manners, was considerable. Actresses now performed women's roles, which hitherto had been played by boys on the London stage, as it was then deemed unseemly for women to act publicly. Movable scenery also came into use along with the proscenium stage in indoor theaters that now replaced the large open-air playhouses like the Globe and Fortune Theatres that had been pulled down.

Licensing continued throughout the Restoration and well into later times. Two acting companies were authorized: the King's Company under Thomas Killigrew and the Duke's Company under Sir William Davenant. Davenant was given the right to perform *King Lear* along with others of Shakespeare's plays, and we know of a performance in January

1664 at Lincoln's Inn Fields and again on June 25, 1675 at the Dorset Garden, a new theater built by Christopher Wren. Although the cast list is unknown, probably Thomas Betterton, the leading actor of the Duke's Company, played Lear, and Mrs. Saunderson, Cordelia.[5]

Shortly thereafter, in 1681, Nahum Tate rewrote Shakespeare's *King Lear*, and it is his version of the play that held the stage in one form or another for the next 150 years. Tate made several drastic changes, not only in the dramatic structure—for example, his play opens with Edmond's soliloquy (Shakespeare's 1.2.1–22)—but in the language and characterizations as well. Taste had changed a good deal from the early decades of the century, and a stricter sense of decorum held the stage. Tate, therefore, eliminated the role of the Fool and introduced a confidante for Cordelia. Most significantly, he altered Shakespeare's ending and restored the more familiar happy conclusion of the sources wherein Cordelia saves her father and restores him to the throne. In another major alteration, Tate had Cordelia and Edgar, who never exchange a word in the original, fall in love, and after many trials and tribulations, they get married at the end.

Much of Shakespeare's language was also revised to conform with the altered taste of the times. Here is a sample of Tate's reworking of Shakespeare's lines, Edmond's opening soliloquy on bastardy:

Thou Nature art my Goddess, to thy law
My Services are bound, why am I then
Depriv'd of a Son's Right, because I came not
In the dull Road that custom has prescrib'd?
Why Bastard, wherefore Base, when I can boast
A Mind as gen'rous, and a Shape as true
As honest Madam's Issue? Why are we
Held Base, who in the lusty stealth of Nature
Take fiercer Qualities than what compound
The scanted Births of the stale Marriage-bed?
Well then, legitimate *Edgar*, to thy right
Of Law I will oppose a Bastard's Cunning.
Our Father's Love is to the Bastard *Edmund*
As to the Legitimate *Edgar*; with success
I've practis'd yet on both their easie Natures:
Here comes the old Man chaf't with th' Information
Which late I forg'd against my Brother *Edgar*,
A Tale so plausible, so boldly utter'd
And heightned by such lucky Accidents,

> That now the slightest circumstance confirms him,
> And Base-born *Edmund* spight of Law inherits.

Tate "regularized" Shakespeare's language and "clarified" it to suit what he saw as the more refined taste of his age. At the same time, he also flattened it. He simplified the subplot and the characters as well. At the start of the play, Edmond's intrigue has already begun, and as Kent and Gloucester enter, Kent tries to intercede on Edgar's behalf, but to no avail. Gloucester is fully convinced by Edmond's treachery, much to Edmond's delight. Edmond in Tate's version is a two-dimensional character, who even tries to assault Cordelia during the course of the action.

Whatever we may think of Tate's redaction, late seventeenth-and eighteenth-century audiences preferred it to Shakespeare's original. Not that Shakespeare's original was entirely eclipsed. Thanks to the efforts of editors beginning with Nicholas Rowe in 1709, his text continued to be reproduced (see chapter 1). But it was not performed; Tate's *King Lear* was. As dissatisfaction with Tate's version began to be registered, however, by the middle of the eighteenth century some actor-managers, preeminently David Garrick, the most celebrated thespian of his age, restored parts of Shakespeare's text, though not his ending. Garrick's script thus contained a mixture of Shakespeare's lines and Tate's, including some interpolated lines, such these by Cordelia, which appear after 4.6.82, when Lear exits:

> *Cordelia* The Gods restore you.
> Hark, I hear afar
> The beaten drum. Old *Kent*'s a man of's word.
> Oh! for an arm
> Like the fierce thunderer's, when the earth-born sons
> Storm'd Heaven, to fight this injur'd father's battle!
> That I cou'd shift my sex, and dye me deep
> In his opposer's blood! But, as I may,
> With women's weapons, piety, and prayers,
> I'll aid his cause.——You never erring Gods,
> Fight on his side, and thunder on his foes
> Such tempests as his poor ag'd head sustain'd:
> Your image suffers, when a monarch bleeds.
> 'Tis your own cause, for that your succours bring;
> Revenge yourselves, and right an injur'd king.

Not until Macready's production in 1838 did the Fool reappear on stage and the original ending return.[6] In America, however, and elsewhere, Tate's *King Lear* or some version of it continued to hold the boards well into the nineteenth century.

King Lear is a very long play, and whether directors use a conflated text, a Q-based, or an F-based one, they are almost bound to make cuts and to have at least a single intermission. Furthermore, the title role is an immense task for any actor to undertake—the "ultimate challenge" for a modern actor, as Hugh Richmond has said.[7] Although cuts in his part do not tend to be many, Shakespeare arranged for a long break in Lear's role after 3.6 to give the actor a chance to recover from the demands on his voice and strength and to prepare for the concluding scenes. More often passages in the Fool's role are cut, such as "Merlin's Prophecy" at the end of 3.2, or some of Kent's lines and Edgar's. Basically actors take one of two approaches to the role of Lear: either he is a titanic personality from the start, or he is a feeble old man. The "strong" and "weak" Lears have been variously played with greater or lesser success.[8]

Because of his size perhaps more than any other reason (he was quite short), David Garrick portrayed Lear as the feeble old man who moved the audience to tears in pity for his distress. His performance, of course, occurred during the Age of Sentiment, when such an interpretation could be counted on for maximum impact, as indeed it did have.[9] By contrast, Tommaso Salvini (1829–1915) was the archetypal titan. Again, his size and bearing may have had much to do with his interpretation, for he was a giant of a man, looking every inch a king, and, as he entered, he towered over his attendants.[10] In more recent productions, such as Laurence Olivier's portrayal for Granada television, or Yuri Yarvet's in Grigori Kozintsev's film, Lear has assumed a more human, rather than titanic, stature. The tendency has been to avoid either extreme of titanism or senility, to fall, that is, within Rosenberg's fourth category. Ian Holm's representation in the Royal National Theatre production at the Cottesloe Theatre, later adapted for television presentation (1999), is perhaps the best recent example of a Lear moving between the very human qualities of a father betrayed by his ungrateful daughters and the outraged king cursing those daughters and promising them the "terrors of the earth."

Other characters also offer interesting variations in the performance of their roles. While Gonerill is almost invariably portrayed as a cold, heartless woman who knows what she is about, as Irene Worth represented her in Peter Brook's production (1962), her sister Regan contrasts against her more or less strongly, depending on the actor's interpretation. At the Royal Shakespeare Theatre in 1993, Sally Dexter played Regan as a very sexy, rather dependent personality, weaker than her older sister but none the less vicious, delighting in a sadistic way at Gloucester's blinding. The most difficult woman's part, however, is doubtless Cordelia's. The actor must resist the temptation to portray her as an entirely self-righteous woman who, recognizing her error, becomes the devoted child in acts 4 and 5. Cordelia is all that and more. Her anxiety as her sisters insincerely protest their love for Lear must seem very real, as must her bitterness in defeat in act 5. Monique Holt, a deaf-mute Korean actress, gave an extraordinary performance of Cordelia at the Shakespeare Theatre in Washington, D.C. in 1999. Using sign language to convey her words, as the Fool spoke her lines, she conveyed the vulnerability as well as the indominatability that is at once at the heart of Cordelia's character. Her slight physical stature and close-cropped, blonde hair coupled with her animated style of acting that stressed her difficulty in making herself clearly understood made this Cordelia all the more appealing.

Another character that has had interesting and quite different representations on the modern stage is the Fool. Ever since Priscilla Horton assumed the role in Macready's production in 1838, a number of female actors have played the Fool, as Emma Thompson and Linda Kerr Scott did in 1990. Thompson's Fool was a mysterious figure in Kenneth Branagh's Renaissance Theatre Company's production, whereas Scott, in the Royal Shakespeare Company's production, despite her strong Glaswegian accent, seemed to capture everything that is close and vulnerable in the Fool's relationship with Lear with her wide eyes, knock-kneed walk, windmilling arms, and desperately comic attempts to bring Lear to his senses. Earlier, in 1982, Antony Sher, making his debut with the RSC, surprised audiences with his outlandish, vaudevillian performance. Carrying a Grock violin and wearing clown's makeup and baggy trousers, he emphasized the influence of Samuel Beckett in Adrian Noble's direction. Together with Michael Gambon, who played Lear, he engaged in occasional cross-talk acts and other vaudeville routines. During the mad trial scene in 3.6, at "Then let them anatomise Regan" (33), Lear plunged his drawn dagger into the Fool, who was standing in an empty oil drum (a vestige apparently from one of Beckett's plays). The dying Fool slowly sank into drum, not to be seen again. This *coup de théâtre* stunned audiences and outraged those critics who preferred to let the ambiguity of Lear's line—"And my poor fool is hanged" (5.3.279)—remain ambiguous.

Although Lear refers to his Fool as "Boy," the character's age is indeterminate; hence, actors of every age have played the part, including some older actors, like David Bradley, in the RSC's 1993 production, and Frank Middlemass in the BBC-TV film. Among some of the most memorable Fools have been Alec McCowen, William Hurt, Jack MacGowran, and John Hurt on stage or on screen.

Set design has frequently been a problem for modern stagings of *King Lear*, though it would not have been at Shakespeare's Globe, which required few props and no movable scenery. The trap in the stage floor would have been sufficient for Edgar's emergence as Tom o'Bedlam in 3.4; no elaborate construction such as the RSC used for Edgar's hovel in the 1990 production is really needed. In the nineteenth century, however, producers like Charles Kean came heavily under the influence of historical authenticity in their attempts to reproduce as faithfully as possible an accurate setting for Shakespeare's plays. Gondolas floated by on real lagoons in productions of *The Merchant of Venice* and *Othello*, and huge castles were mounted on stage for the English history plays and *Hamlet*. Since the actual time of King Lear fades into prehistory, one cannot be sure what kind of setting would most closely approximate his era. Kean, therefore, chose to set his production in the Anglo-Saxon period of about A.D. 800, the closest period, that is, for which he could find some reliable and definite information on settings and costumes, but sufficiently remote in time.

More recent productions have eschewed historical accuracy in favor of a timeless setting or, as in Peter Brook's 1962 RSC production, which Brook himself designed, a setting that conveyed "very harsh, cruel and realistic situations."[11] In his film version of the play, Brook went on location in Denmark's Jutland to capture a primitive landscape, but, for at least one viewer, that harsh, primitive setting seemed incongruous with the fine blank verse most characters spoke. By contrast, Grigori Kozintsev updated his setting to the Christian era, thus making the allusions to the gospels that appear in the play more appropriate and less anachronistic. Modern dress productions, such as one directed by Trevor Nunn in 1976, have sometimes also been staged. Nunn chose the period of World War I as his setting, the last era, he believed, in which a sovereign could behave as Lear does.[12] The rest of this chapter will concentrate in detail on several noteworthy twentieth-century productions both on stage

and on film or videotape. For productions up to 1982 I am heavily in-
debted to Alexander Leggatt's volume on the play in the *Shakespeare in
Performance* series published by Manchester University Press.

PETER BROOK AND THE ROYAL SHAKESPEARE COMPANY, 1962

Peter Brook was still a young director, known for his controversial
productions of Shakespeare's plays that sought for, and invariably found,
novel approaches to the canon. He already had an interesting track record
with his stagings of *Love's Labor's Lost* and *Titus Andronicus* when he
decided to tackle *King Lear* for the Royal Shakespeare Company, using
Paul Scofield in the title role. Eschewing elaborate settings, his sets con-
sisted basically of three white walls and some rough furniture—Lear's
throne, for example, with no ornate trappings around it, and an astrological chart in 1.2 to reflect Gloucester's comments on "these late eclipses
of the sun and moon" and Edmond's response to his father's superstitiousness. The most unusual prop was a set of three large rusted thun-
dersheets clearly visible on stage for the storm scenes. Finding the sight
of these vibrating sheets somehow disturbing, Brook decided to put the
thunder, as it were, on view, their vibrations activated by hidden motors.
Costumes were also quite simple, further suggesting a primitive era. The
men, including Lear after the opening scene, wore leather coats and
boots, and women wore long gowns with little or no jewelry or other
decoration. The "visual shock" of the production was so surprising that
some reviewers became confused, but the impact upon audiences was
profound.[13]

Brook was determined from the first not to offer a popular *Lear*, that
is, a version of the play that inspired easy emotional responses (if that
is ever possible with a play like *King Lear*), or one that evoked traditional sympathy for a man "more sinned against than sinning." Not that
the production lacked emotional power; but it was aimed more at the
head than the heart, as some of Brook's textual cuts indicate. For instance, Brook followed the Folio in deleting the dialogue between Cornwall's servants at the end of act 3 that voices compassion for Gloucester
and contempt for Cornwall and Regan. Brook also cut the the lines near
the end of act 5 when Edmond has a change of heart and tries to save
Cordelia. Critics have maintained that Brook was heavily influenced by
Jan Kott's essay, *"King Lear*, or *Endgame"* in *Shakespeare Our Contemporary* (1964), which analyzed Shakespeare's play in light of Samuel

Beckett's theater of the absurd, and clearly Brook's production had strong affinities with Beckett. But this influence was more apparent in the film version Brook later directed (see below), which was far more heavily cut and presented a much more bleak interpretation.

Paul Scofield's King Lear was, by all accounts, outstanding. His was by no means a traditional Lear, complete with long white hair and beard. He was, according to Leggatt, who saw the original production at Stratford-upon-Avon, "a tough, wiry, still vigorous old man."[14] His voice more than anything else about him stood out: harsh, crusty, "a sound like grinding rocks."[15] He did not easily arouse sympathy. In 1.4, on Lear's return from hunting, his calls for dinner and his fool were reinforced by loud repetitions by his knights, a noisy, rowdy lot that fully justified Gonerill's complaints against them. Indeed, Brook tried hard to show that the wicked sisters and Edmond had a rational point of view that finds support, though not emphasis, in the text. And none of that makes it easy to feel sorry for the king.

Alec McCowen's Fool, similarly, did not play for pathos. "His salient feature was intellectual sharpness. . . . He could be frightened, bitter, angry," but his concern for Lear was uppermost.[16] Alan Webb as Gloucester presented, at first, a fussy old man, a trimmer who sought the line of least resistance until that became intolerable even for him. His blinding was the moment of extremest cruelty in the play, forcing some audience members to exit in sheer horror at what was being staged. Bound to a chair overturned backwards, his legs in the air, he submitted helplessly to Cornwall, who used his spur to extract first one eye and then the other. But the moment of greatest pathos came not at the end of this scene, when the servants casually push him offstage to let him "smell his way to Dover," but later, on Dover Beach, when he meets the mad king, pulls off his boots, and harkens to his preaching while emitting tearless sobs.

All directors make sure that the differences among the three daughters, especially Gonerill and Regan, are clear, and Brook was no exception. Gonerill is traditionally the stronger of the two wicked daughters, and Irene Worth was certainly that. More difficult is the portrayal of Cordelia, enacted by Diana Rigg, who played her not as the gentle, sweet, misunderstood young woman, as she so often appears, but as the coolly self-contained, intelligent, and determined person she is, at least at the beginning of the play.

Following the transfer to London from Stratford, the production went on tour to Eastern Europe and Moscow, where it was an unprecedented

success. Audiences were moved not by the image of an old father betrayed by his daughters so much as by Lear as "the figure of old Europe,
tired, and feeling, as almost every country in Europe does, that after the
events of the last fifty years people have borne enough."[17] Indeed, the
image of King Lear transcends ordinary humanity in that, as in other
ways, though the human dimension cannot be ignored or eliminated in
the process. When the tour came to America, however, the production
went flat. Whether this was the result of the actors going stale after
performing so long (it was now more than two years since its first performances), or whether the audience reactions could scarcely replicate
those the company found in Europe, is hard to say. Certainly, a live
production is always influenced by its audiences, and North American
audiences had nothing like the experiences of the Europeans to bring to
the theater. They could hardly be expected to respond similarly.

Half a dozen years later, Brook decided to film *King Lear* at the same
time that Grigori Kozintsev, the great Russian director, was making his
own film version. The two films could hardly be more unlike each other
(see below). Brook went to Jutland in Denmark to film, where he found
the bleak, barren landscape more appropriate for what he wanted to
show. The cast included many of the same actors as in the stage production: Paul Scofield, Alan Webb, Irene Worth, but a different Cordelia,
whose role was cut to the barest minimum in an interpretation that allowed for little or no relief from unremitting cruelty and destructiveness.

In films, we are accustomed to background music that more often than
not emphasizes, if it does not directly induce, the audience's emotional
response to the action displayed on screen. Perhaps this is one reason
Brook included no music whatsoever in his film, apart from the Fool's
songs and some "strange electronic noises in the storm."[18] But, though
severely cut, this was not a minimalist *King Lear*. From the opening
scene, during which the camera panned across scores of silent, watchful
faces of a crowd standing in expectation of a momentous event, to the
end at Dover Beach, where Cordelia's ships burned and destruction was
everywhere, Brook expanded his production, using the resources of film
where he found them most useful for his purpose. For example, at the
end of scene 1.4, Lear and his Fool hurry away from Gonerill's palace
in a crude carriage over the primitive landscape, and 1.5 takes place,
accordingly, inside the carriage's compartment.

The primitiveness that Brook wanted and displayed in Jutland appeared strangely incongruous with the sophisticated blank verse of the
dialogue. But unlike Kozintsev, who chose to use Boris Pasternak's free

translation of Shakespeare, Brook rejected the script Ted Hughes had prepared for him and retained Shakespeare's dialogue, except for the many cuts he made. Here, he followed the example of other Shakespeare films, which translate verbal imagery into visual. He also transposed a number of scenes, moving 1.2 to a point after 1.5, for example, and chopped others into shorter segments, following the precedents set by Olivier's *Hamlet* (1949) and other Shakespeare films. The result is a quite different rendering of the play, in no way a reproduction of the stage version, but a new, filmic interpretation that some felt did violence to Shakespeare's text but others found a powerful adaptation of it. The scene at Dover Beach where Lear preaches to the blinded Gloucester sitting before him is extremely moving, and the clips of Lear's slowly descending head at the end make good use of film technology. One startling interpolation is Gonerill's death, which in the play occurs off-stage. In Brook's film we see her swaying from side to side gathering more speed, shaking her head as she does so, and then smashing it against a stone boulder.

GRIGORI KOZINTSEV'S RUSSIAN LANGUAGE FILM (1970)

Although filmed at the same time as Brook's *King Lear*, Kozintsev's had an earlier release date. Its North American premiere was at the first World Shakespeare Congress in Vancouver, British Columbia, in August 1971, where it received a standing ovation from 500 assembled delegates, including many of the most renowned Shakespearean scholars and critics. Some had already seen Brook's film and felt that the contrast between the two versions could not have been greater. Where Brook gave a stronger emphasis than his stage production to the absurdist aspects he saw in *King Lear*, shearing away every suggestion of optimistic humanism, Kozintsev presented *King Lear* in the grand manner of his Russian predecessors, such as Eisenstein, but revealing, as he did so, the socialist implications he found in Shakespeare's text.

From the very start of the film, Kozintsev's socialist bias is apparent. Where Brook used the camera to pan across the faces of a multitude, Kozintsev used it to show hordes of poor people, their feet bound in rags, moving along a dirt road. These are the "poor naked wretches" that Lear will later come in contact with in the storm scene; for Shakespeare's hovel, in this film, becomes a shelter accommodating a large number of these same poor folk for whom Lear, himself now wretched, begins to feel some sympathy.[19] But despite this socialist bias, or perhaps because of it, the setting is not pre-Christian Britain. As the people move over the landscape, we see tombs with crosses and other symbols of Christianity, as when Edgar kneels and prays over his father's grave. Religion, no more than monarchy, has not done its proper job in alleviating the condition of the poor of the earth.

This movement of the people, followed by knights riding on horseback, then Kent and Gloucester walking together, all combine to convey a sense of "Lear's relentless journey," as Kozintsev conceived it, which does not end till his life ends.[20] As in Brook's film, liberties are taken with the text. Lear enters in 1.1 together with his Fool, with whom he has been playing. Yuri Yarvet's Lear is the antithesis of Scofield's: shorter, far more frail, he is the elderly father, not the powerful monarch who gives away his kingdom. He does have moments of rage, as when he furiously shakes the map of his kingdom after Cordelia fails to please him, and later when he appears on his castle walls to proclaim Cordelia's banishment, while his subjects fall to their knees. But Yarvet's Lear is what Kozintsev wanted: not an extraordinary king but an everyman, "whose reduction to common humanity would be not the end of his greatness but the beginning of it."[21] This is the ultimate goal of his journey, as Kozintsev conceived it.

Where Brook blurred the distinctions between good and evil, lending weight to Gonerill and Regan's point of view and Edmond's, Kozintsev stressed the moral sense of Shakespeare's play, as he saw it: learning leading to redemption, and the triumph of good over evil. Not that the triumph comes without tragic cost, or that the strugggle exists without cruelty and violence. This would return the play to something like Nahum Tate's redaction. Kozintsev retains the tragic elements, but extends them beyond the personal to encompass the social in as broad terms as possible. He also retains some of the absurdity—as in the train of possessions Lear selects to accompany him on his initial journey out of Gonerill's palace—but without the overriding emphasis that Brook gives it.[22] Both the social and the absurdist aspects are there in Shakespeare's text, but they can be more or less evident as the director interprets their significance.

Where Brook eschewed any music whatsoever, Kozintsev again commissioned Dimitri Shostakovitch to compose a score for this film as he had done for his film of *Hamlet*, but with this difference: he did not want to use "themes." He preferred more sweeping sounds, as in the war sequence, where his wordless choir voiced the people's grief over what was happening to their country.[23] He eliminated Gloucester's suicidal "leap," perhaps because he did not wish to stress the theme of despair, or because he felt that it depended too heavily on theatrical conventions not available to film.[24] But he does show Gloucester's death upon recognizing his son Edgar and dying of joy. By contrast, he presented the death of Cordelia far more brutally, hanging in an archway near the wall on which Lear, as at the beginning of the film when he banished her, emits his blood-curdling cries, "Howl, howl, howl, howl, howl!" After she is cut down, his repetition of "never" emphasizes the finality of their separation in death.

The film does not end there. As the bodies of Lear and Cordelia are carried off together on a stretcher, the three survivors—Albany, Kent, and Edgar—look on, affirming, in a way, the ultimate triumph of good. The moment is not sentimentalized, for, as the soldiers bear the litter on its way, the Fool, who has never disappeared, is seen again, playing on his pipe as earlier in the film. As the soldiers pass him, one of them kicks him out of the way, a gesture that makes its own statement about the Lear world. At the very end, Edgar approaches the camera to speak the final lines. But they are not said. Kozintsev depended on Leonard Merzin's facial expression, and especially his eyes, to express what Shakespeare's words tried to do, perhaps inadequately, even for Shakespeare.

ADRIAN NOBLE AND THE ROYAL SHAKESPEARE COMPANY (1982)

Adrian Noble was the first director at the RSC to attempt *King Lear* after Peter Brook's momentous production twenty years earlier, a production that remained vivid in the memories of many theatergoers and critics. Noble therefore felt he had to do something quite different, and he did. Although, like Brook's, his production was heavily influenced by the theater of the absurd and particularly the plays of Samuel Beckett, neither the sets, nor the costumes, nor anything else resembled Brook's production. Michael Gambon played Lear and Antony Sher, the Fool. What was most startling about their performance was the interpolation of vaudeville routines occasionally in their dialogue. Sher adopted the costume of a Beckettian clown, with a red nose and Grock violin, baggy trousers, battered trilby hat, and greatly oversized shoes. The effect was astonishing, as it was intended to be.

Gambon's Lear was the strong titan that his physique as well as his voice clearly conveyed. His powerful presence dominated the scenes in which he appeared, as when he cursed Gonerill, who visibly trembled at his vehemence. The question became, as Leggatt puts it, "whether this oak-like Lear could change."[25] Critics divided on this, some finding that, lacking inwardness, he tended to remain the same strong figure as in the opening scenes; others saw in his suffering features a great depth of misery, suggesting the purgatory he was experiencing that foreshadowed his resurgent humanity.[26] Perhaps the most unusual scene occurred during the storm, which Noble staged in a novel fashion. As the winds blew, Lear and the Fool stood on a small platform at the end of a ten-foot pole, hugging each other—quite desperately where Sher was concerned— as they swayed back and forth in the fierce elements raging about them.

If the production lacked design coherence, which many felt it did, this seems to have been deliberate. Noble opted for an eclecticism rarely seen in such productions, and was perhaps prompted to some of his innovations and the production's political slant by staging Edward Bond's *Lear* at the RSC's The Other Place during the same run. The first scenes suggested a Renaissance milieu, but these quickly gave place to a Russian or even Oriental—I thought Tibetan—setting. Noble seemed to be bringing the action closer and closer to our own time, as when Oswald appeared in 1.3 in a simple modern uniform carrying an attaché case, or when Lear later during the storm and on Dover Beach wore a waistcoat, trousers, and short sleeves.[27] Water in the form of a stream, in which Lear and Gloucester bathed their feet, actually passed over the forestage during the Dover Beach scene. One of Lear's boots remained behind afterwards, a symbol (as some regarded it) from Beckett's plays. The battle scene was far from subdued. This was 1982, and Britain was at war over the Falklands, as Noble was fully aware. He brought the horrors of modern warfare directly on stage.

A decade later, in 1993, Noble again staged *King Lear* for the Royal Shakespeare Company, with Robert Stephens as Lear. This was a completely different production. Most of the eclectism of 1982 was gone and in its place, a more consistent if somewhat modernized setting. Costumes suggested the late eighteenth century, a time of revolution in Europe and of Blake's opposition of Reason and Energy, as Lois Potter saw it.[28] The stage set was dominated for the whole first half—up to the end of act 3—by a huge globe suspended over the action which, as Gloucester moved slowly off stage, opened and dropped a large amount of sand, as if nature's molds had indeed cracked and all germens were spilling at once before our eyes (see 3.2.8). This seemed too literal a representation of the verse for some in the audience, however much it impressed others.

Stephens as Lear, at least on his good nights, was profoundly moving, capturing every nuance and change in the king, from the proud majesty at the beginning to the "foolish fond old man" at the end of act 4. He seemed to embody and project throughout his performance Lear's "I gave you all" (2.4.243). Or, as one theatrical reviewer said, "I can re-member no performance of the role in which an actor gave so much of himself,"[29] a view with which I heartily concur. Stephens was ill before and intermittently during the run of the play; actually, he had not much longer to live, though he possibly could not have known this. At any rate, one could not help but be moved by his performance as, in a quite different way, we were two years earlier when he enacted Falstaff in the *Henry IV* plays, also directed by Noble.

As in Kozintsev's film, the Fool made his appearance from the very beginning, but Ian Hughes's Fool in Noble's production was quite dif-ferent from Oleg Dal's. He entered wearing a red blindfold, and marked out the various divisions of the kingdom as each daughter proclaimed her love for the king. The blindfold apparently symbolized the blindness theme in the play, here Lear's wilful blindness and later Gloucester's physical blindness (hence the red blindfold). Diminutive as he was, he was not like Dal's boyish, shaven-headed Fool, but wore a red military-style coat and acted very deliberately and rationally. This King Lear did not kill his Fool in 3.6, as Gambon did; instead, after the mock trial was over, Hughes just picked up Lear's knife and walked off with it, not to be seen again. Potter may be right when she comments: "Perhaps he was going to anatomize himself to find out why he had stayed with the king so long, against all that reason told him. The reason for his death seemed to be simply that the play, as it lurches into complete irrationality, has no room for him any more."[30]

Noble was fortunate once more in having an excellent supporting cast for his production. Owen Teale as Kent protected Lear on stage as he did off, and David Bradley, who had played the Fool in Deborah War-ner's 1990 production at the Royal National Theatre, was a thoroughly convincing Gloucester. Simon Russell Beale enacted Edgar and staged his development from naive *vir bonus* ("good man") to vigorous avenger against his brother with all the sensitivity the part requires, as when he gently placed the blind Gloucester's hand in Lear's at Dover Beach. At the end, Lear does not ask those on stage or off to look at Cordelia's lips but at her spirit, which he believes he sees ascending heavenward. Potter aptly explains the significance of this interpretation: Lear's lines are completed by Edgar's final speech. "We"—the audience as well as the survivors left on stage—"shall never see so much" as Lear has just claimed to see; our world view is not or cannot be his.[31]

RICHARD EYRE AND THE ROYAL NATIONAL THEATRE (BBC-TV, 1999)

Although *King Lear* seems to demand huge space for its presentation, Richard Eyre chose the small studio theater in the National Theatre complex, the Cottesloe, for his production with Ian Holm in the leading role. It was an immense success and was later adapted for television by the BBC and shown in the United States and elsewhere. It is this televised version, recorded on videotape, that is the basis for discussion here.

Except for the storm scenes, which were very realistically presented with real rain pouring down on those out in the weather, and the brief battle scene, Eyre retained much of the look of the original Cottesloe set: simple, bare walls and corridors prevailed, with no extraordinary lighting effects. The emphasis was clearly on the actors and the language they spoke, not spectacle, just as some Shakespearean purists insist it should be. Close-ups were of course used to great effect—this is the greatest advantage of film or videotape over stage presentation, though it suffers from the correlative disadvantage of selecting what the audience will see and not allowing us to view the entire action taking place on stage. Ian Holm was once more outstanding in his enactment of the king and had a first-rate supporting cast.

Like Yuri Yarvet in Kozintsev's film, Holm is a man small of stature, though big of heart, and by no means frail; and this is how he played King Lear. Already in his late sixties, Holm was still vigorous, and his close-cropped hair and beard still showed signs of grey. His fury, when it broke out, could be terrifying enough; certainly it shocked his daughters when he hurled his curses at Gonerill in 1.4. But he modulated his voice, so that at times when Lear finds it prudent to speak calmly he could interrupt his anger and speak more softly. For example, when Lear considers momentarily at 2.4.98–105 that Regan and Cornwall may have good reason for not wishing to see him just then, Holm's voice softened, but then he broke out into a rage immediately afterwards when he saw Kent in the stocks. Holm's most moving scene was unquestionably the reconciliation with Cordelia at the end of act 4, aided by Amanda Redman's beautiful portrayal of his daughter. At first still mad, he cries out loudly that he is bound upon a wheel of fire; but then he begins to recover. He knows he is ill and suffering, as he tests his finger on a pin Cordelia wears, and gently touches her face to feel the tears that begin to stream from her eyes. Slight as he is, Holm could still carry his dead daughter in his arms at the end.

Eyre did not cut the text with a machete, but used a scalpel instead. Speeches are shortened, but few scenes were eliminated or transposed. Edgar's soliloquy in 2.3 was reduced to its last line only, and 3.1 was deleted altogether. Kent does not open a letter from Cordelia at the end of 2.2 to read and find some comfort in it, and Edgar's lines at the beginning of 4.1 are cut, also. That scene begins with the Old Man leading the blinded Gloucester; Edgar's reactions to this sight are conveyed by his facial expression, not words. This recalls Kozintsev's direction at the end of his film when he did not have Edgar speak the last lines. Eyre did not cut Edgar's final speech, however; it is spoken as Kent wheels the wagon carrying the dead bodies of Lear and his daughter off into an enveloping fog.

Eyre did much at the beginning to show the elder daughters' dismay at Lear's treatment of them. Gonerill especially appears to have a case against her father, whose knights are shown to be as unruly in 1.4 as the small set permitted. When Lear turns on her, she fairly quakes, but holds firm nevertheless. Amidst repressed sobs she later explains her rationale to her husband, Albany, who seems skeptical; he is a stronger figure than we are used to seeing. Regan is a sexy blonde, who refuses her arm to her wounded husband in 3.7 and loses no time in making a play for Edmond. The rivalry between the daughters for his favor is pronounced; at the beginning of 4.2, Gonerill and Edmond exchange passionate kisses even as Albany approaches and sees them. In Eyre's presentation, this rivalry perhaps more than anything leads to the daughters' destruction.

In the opening scene, Lear makes a great show of affection towards all of his daughters, but especially Regan and Cordelia, as if to suggest the theme of incest that some commentators believe underlies Lear's actions. Lear wraps his arms around each daughter before she speaks and kisses Cordelia on the top of her head. Regan returns the affection and, rising from the conference table around which they are all seated, hugs her father as she begins her speech. Cordelia remains seated and, with tears in her eyes, nonetheless forthrightly answers "Nothing" when Lear asks what she can say to get a better share of the kingdom. Dark haired and comely, obviously younger than her sisters, she elicits an immediate sympathy. Looking very much like Lear until he dons his disguise (essentially a wig of long dark hair and a commoner's accent), Kent intercedes on her behalf, but Lear has no patience with him, climbing on the table to banish his insubordinate vassal.

Her dress stained with tears, Cordelia begs Lear to explain to Burgundy (played by a black actor) and the king of France (also dark, but not negroid) what she has done to deserve his wrath. When France later tells her to bid farewell to her sisters, she angrily denounces them and wins their contempt. When she reappears in act 4, we first see her amidst many candles praying, as Kent and the Gentleman speak some of their lines in 4.3 as a voice-over. She is in armor in the next scene, sending soldiers out to find her father, but in later scenes she is once again simply dressed.

Neither set nor costumes in this production convey any specific epoch, although the explosions in the battle scene suggest that the period is closer to our time than to the historical period of King Lear. Swords are used in the duel between Edgar and Edmond, but otherwise the events could occur at almost any time. At the beginning of the tape, we watch an eclipse of the sun by the moon as the credits roll, but no astrological chart appears, as in the Brook stage production, to suggest an earlier era fraught with superstition. The storm scenes are convincing enough, and all of the characters out in the storm are thoroughly soaked through.

One of the most interesting representations in this production is that of the Fool, played by Michael Bryant, a man of about the same age as Holm. He comes on in 1.4 almost unnoticed during the furor, wearing a simple quilted jacket and a pointed hat, or cap. This is a merry Fool at first, joking and singing his songs, trying to make Lear laugh, but not withholding the point of his satire and his quips. By the storm scenes, however, he is almost done in; therefore, his disappearance afterwards is not surprising. In fact, his last line, "And I will go to bed at noon," is very much a valediction. He is reincarnated, after a fashion, in Lear during the Dover Beach scenes, as signalled by his hat, which reappears on Lear's head. There is no ambiguity about who is hanged at the end, for Cordelia has a noose around her when Lear carries her in, and the bond between her and the Fool is never emphasized.

The Gloucester plot is curtailed but not by much; in fact, after the opening shots of the eclipse, we see Edgar busily writing down notes with a book open before him, as Edmond looks on. Edmond's soliloquy from 1.2 begins here and continues later, after 1.1 begins. He remains an observer of the action throughout that scene, overhearing Gonerill and

Regan at the end of it plotting against their father. He is as sinister-looking as Edgar is innocent, and quickly attracts the attention of Regan, when she sees him in 2.1, and Gonerill in 3.7. By this time, whatever ambiguity Eyre has developed in the sisters' attitude to their father has been resolved into a hardened wickedness, underscored by their sexual rivalry regarding Edmond. The duel between the two brothers is vigorous enough, with Edgar emerging victorious after a few close calls when Edmond almost does him in. His speech describing Gloucester's death and Kent's condition is cut; but Edmond, grimly smiling when he sees Gonerill and Regan dead, is allowed to try to save Cordelia with his dying breath.

Lear dies in Edgar's arms, looking upward (like Stephens's Lear) at what he seems to think is Cordelia's spirit flying heavenward, a wan smile on his face. But the final shot of Kent wheeling the wagon out into the fog with the bodies of Lear and his daughters does not allow the audience to feel that this is in any way a happy ending for Lear or for any of the survivors. The eldest have borne most, as Edgar says, and the audience feels that most acutely.

NOTES

1. *Shakespearean Tragedy*, 3d ed. (London: Macmillan, 1992), p. 211.

2. On the composition of the King's Men and the doubling of Cordelia and the Fool, see William A. Ringler Jr., "Shakespeare and His Actors: Some Remarks on *King Lear*," in *Shakespeare's Art from a Comparative Perspective*, ed. Wendell M. Aycock (1981), pp. 187–93. See also Richard Abrams, "The Double Casting of Cordelia and Lear's Fool: A Theatrical View," *Texas Studies in Literature and Language* 27 (1985), 354–68, and Giorgio Melchiori, "Peter, Balthasar, and Shakespeare's Art of Doubling," *Modern Language Review* 78 (1983), 777–92.

3. See R. Chris Hassel Jr., *Renaissance Drama and the English Church Year* (Lincoln: University of Nebraska Press, 1979), pp. 22–30.

4. The play was performed in 1610 at Gowthwaite Hall in Yorkshire by a provincial acting company under the protection of Sir Richard Cholmeley. See C. J. Sisson, "Shakespeare's Quartos as Prompt-Copies, with Some Account of Cholmeley's Players and a New Shakespeare Allusion," *Review of English Studies* 18 (1942), 129–43.

5. In his University of Texas doctoral dissertation, "The Stage History of *King Lear*," Leland Eugene Derrick speculates on these and other actors' roles in this production. He does not consider doubling of the Fool and Cordelia but lists James Nokes as the Fool.

6. Macready actually began using Shakespeare's ending a few years earlier, in 1834. Edmund Kean in 1823 tried to restore it, but after several performances was forced to return to Tate's.

7. "A Letter to the Actor Playing Lear," in *Shakespearean Illuminations: Essays in Honor of Marvin Rosenberg*, ed. Jay L. Halio and Hugh Richmond (Newark: University of Delaware Press, 1998), p. 110.

8. See Marvin Rosenberg, *The Masks of King Lear* (1972; reprint, Newark: University of Delaware Press, 1992), pp. 22–32. Rosenberg suggests two further models: Lear from the start as a slightly mad or senile old man, and Lear as a man who moves between the extremes of the "august king" and the "very human father driven to madness," avoiding the extremes of either of the first two archetypes and emphasizing "the human qualities staining the imperial marble." He cites Ludwig Max Devrient (1784–1832), the greatest German Lear, as an example of the former type, and William Charles Macready (1793–1873) as an example of the latter.

9. Alexander Leggatt, *Shakespeare in Performance: "King Lear"* (Manchester: Manchester University Press, 1991), p. 8.

10. Rosenberg, *Masks*, p. 22.

11. Leggat, p. 34, citing Brook's *The Shifting Point* (New York: Harper and Row, 1987), p. 88.

12. See J. S. Bratton, ed., *King Lear* (Plays in Performance) (Bristol: Bristol Classical Plays, 1987), p. 62.

13. See Leggatt, p. 36, for an account of reactions.

14. Ibid., p. 47.

15. Ibid.

16. Ibid., p. 41.

17. Peter Brook, *The Shifting Point* (1987), cited by Leggatt, p. 51.

18. Leggatt, p. 97.

19. As Leggatt notes (p. 82), Shakespeare's text includes no place for the poor to appear on stage, but for Kozintsev "one cannot portray the life of a king without portraying the life of his subjects" (Kozintsev, *King Lear: The Space of Tragedy* (1977), cited by Leggatt).

20. Leggatt, pp. 80–81.

21. Ibid., p. 89, citing Kozintsev, *Space of Tragedy*, p. 11.

22. Ibid., pp. 88–89.

23. Ibid., p. 91.

24. See Leggatt, pp. 90–91.

25. Ibid., p. 74.

26. See Leggatt, pp. 74–75, for a summary of divergent views.

27. Ibid., p. 69.

28. Lois Potter, "Macready, the Two-Text Theory, and the RSC's 1993 *King Lear*," in *Critical Essays on "King Lear,"* ed. Jay L. Halio (New York: G. K. Hall, 1996), p. 210.

29. Irving Wardle, *The Independent on Sunday*, 23 May 1993; cited by Potter, p. 215, n. 19.

30. Potter, p. 213.

31. Ibid., p. 214.

SELECTED BIBLIOGRAPHY

EDITIONS

Bevington, David, ed. *King Lear*. New York: Bantam Books, 1988. A conflated text with supplementary materials on sources.

Foakes, R. A., ed. *King Lear*. Third Arden edition. Walton-on-Thames, Surrey: Thomas Nelson, 1997. A fully annotated, conflated text, with quarto- and F-only passages designated by superscript Q or F.

Halio, Jay L., *The First Quarto of "King Lear."* Cambridge: Cambridge University Press, 1994. A quarto-based edition with textual introduction and notes and collation, but no commentary.

Halio, Jay L., ed. *King Lear*. New Cambridge Shakespeare. Cambridge: Cambridge University Press, 1992. Fully annotated, Folio-based text, with quarto-only passages in an appendix.

Warren, Michael, ed. *The Complete "King Lear," 1608–1623*. Berkeley and Los Angeles: University of California Press, 1989. Facsimile reproductions of Q1, Q2, and F, plus a a separate parallel Q1 and F text, showing both the corrected and uncorrected states of each. Includes a general introduction and annotated bibliography.

Weis, René, ed. *King Lear: A Parallel Text edition*. London: Longmans, 1993. In modern-spelling with quarto and Folio on facing pages and notes below.

Wells, Stanley, ed. *King Lear*. Oxford: Oxford University Press, 2000. A fully annotated, quarto-based edition, with F-only passages noted in the collation. Gary Taylor prepared the text.

TEXTUAL STUDIES

Blayney, Peter W. M. *The Texts of "King Lear" and Their Origins*, 2 vols. Cambridge: Cambridge University Press, 1982. Only volume 1 so far

has been published. It contains an excellent account of the printing of
the First Quarto.

Greg, W. W. *The Shakespeare First Folio: Its Bibliographical and Textual History*. Oxford: Clarendon Press, 1955. A good survey of textual problems, comparing both Q and F texts.

——*The Variants in the First Quarto of "King Lear."*Oxford: Clarendon Press, 1940. Still the standard on the subject.

Hinman, Charlton. *The Printing and Proofreading of the First Folio of Shakespeare*. 2 vols. Oxford: Clarendon Press, 1963. A breakthrough study showing how the Folio was printed and corrected. Hinman was the first to identify Compositor E, who set much of *King Lear*, as an apprentice.

Ioppolo, Grace. *Revising Shakespeare*. Cambridge, Mass.: Harvard University Press, 1991. Contains an important section on *King Lear* regarding the revision of the role of Cordelia.

Taylor, Gary, and Michael Warren, eds. *The Division of the Kingdoms: Shakespeare's Two Versions of "King Lear."* Oxford: Clarendon Press, 1983. Contains a dozen essays, including an introduction by Stanley Wells endorsing the two-text theory.

Urkowitz, Stephen. *Shakespeare's Revision of "King Lear."* Princeton: Princeton University Press, 1980. A thorough study of Shakespeare's revisions.

Warren, Michael. "Quarto and Folio *King Lear* and the Interpretation of Albany and Edgar," in *Shakespeare: Pattern of Excelling Nature*, ed. David Bevington and Jay L. Halio. Newark: University of Delaware Press, 1978, pp. 95–107. Shows how F revised the roles of these two characters from their appearance in Q.

SOURCES AND CONTEXTS

Bullough, Geoffrey. *Narrative and Dramatic Sources of Shakespeare*. 8 vols. New York: Columbia University Press, 1957–75. Vol. 7 (1973) contains the materials pertinent to *King Lear*.

de Mendonça, Barbara Heliodora Carneiro. "The Influences of *Gorboduc* on *King Lear*," *Shakespeare Survey* 13 (1960): 41–48. Shows how the early chronicle play may have influenced Shakespeare's composition.

Elton, William R. *"King Lear" and the Gods*. 2nd ed. Lexington: University Press of Kentucky, 1988. Places *King Lear* in the context of classical and Christian ideas, concluding that Shakespeare's play does not support Christian interpretations.

Hamilton, Donna. "Some Romance Sources for *King Lear*," in *Studies in Philology* 71 (1974): 173–92. On the parallel story of King Robert of Sicily.

Hardison, O. B. "Myth and History in *King Lear*," in *Shakespeare Quarterly* 26 (1975): 227–42. On the classical influences in *King Lear*, especially the myth of Ixion.

Honan, Park. *Shakespeare: A Life*. Oxford: Oxford University Press, 1998. A major biography that places the plays in the context of Shakespeare's working life.

Kinney, Arthur F. "Some Conjectures on the Composition of *King Lear*," *Shakespeare Survey* 33 (1980): 13–25. Considers the influence of William Jones's translation of Lipsius's *Six Bookes of Politickes or Ciuill Doctrine* (1594) on the political and philosophical thought in *King Lear*.

Miola, Robert. *Shakespeare's Reading*. Oxford: Oxford University Press, 2000. On pp. 109–16 Miola Analyzes Shakespeare's use of his sources in *King Lear*.

Muir, Kenneth. "Samuel Harsnett and *King Lear*," *Review of English Studies* 2 (1951): 11–21. Shows how Shakespeare borrowed from Harsnett for Edgar's idiom as Tom o'Bedlam.

Perrett, Wilfrid. *The King Lear Story from Geoffrey of Monmouth to Shakespeare*. Berlin, 1904; reprint, New York: Johnson Reprint, 1970. Comments on two dozen or more folktales most pertinent to the study of *King Lear*, as well as Geoffrey's *History*.

Shaheen, Naseeb. *Biblical References in Shakespeare's Plays*. Newark: University of Delaware Press, 1999. A compendium of biblical references and analogues, with some critical analysis.

Snyder, Susan. "*King Lear* and the Prodigal Son," *Shakespeare Quarterly* 17 (1966): 361–69. Considers the play in the context of the biblical story of the Prodigal Son.

Welsford, Enid. *The Fool: His Social and Literary History*. 1935; reprint, Garden City, N.Y.: Doubleday, 1961. Provides excellent background for understanding the Fool in *King Lear*.

Wittreich, Joseph. "*Image of that Horror": History, Prophecy, and Apocalypse in "King Lear."* San Marino, Calif.: Huntington Library, 1984. Draws attention to the prophetic center and apocalyptic framework of *King Lear*.

GENERAL CRITICISM

Bloom, Harold. *Shakespeare: The Invention of the Human*. New York: Riverhead Books, 1998. Written from the standpoint of liberal humanism, the chapter on *King Lear* is one of the best essays written on the play.

Booth, Stephen. "*King Lear," "Macbeth," and Indefinition and Tragedy*. New Haven: Yale University Press, 1983. Particularly good on the "false endings" in *King Lear*.

Bradley, A. C. *Shakespearean Tragedy*. 3rd. ed. London: Macmillan, 1992. Originally published in 1904 and many times reprinted, a standard treatment of the subject. Besides chapters on *King Lear* and three other major

tragedies, it contains an introductory chapter on aspects of Shakespearean
    tragedy that remains pertinent and useful.

Bruce, Susan. *William Shakespeare: "King Lear."* New York: Columbia Uni-
    versity Press, 1998. Surveys the range of Shakespearean criticism from
    neo-classicism and romanticism to the present.

Colie, Rosalie L. and F. T. Flahiff. *Some Facets of "King Lear": Essays in
    Prismatic Criticism,* eds. Toronto: University of Toronto Press, 1974.
    Contains a dozen excellent essays, including F. D. Hoeniger's on "The
    Artist Exploring the Primitive: *King Lear,*" all from a variety of critical
    approaches.

Cunningham, J. V. *Woe or Wonder: The Emotional Effect of Shakespearean
    Tragedy.* 1951; reprint, Denver: Alan Swallow, 1964. Explains the mean-
    ing of "Ripeness is all."

Danby, John F. *Shakespeare's Doctrine of Nature: A Study of "King Lear"*
    London: Faber and Faber, 1948. A thorough examination of the many
    different conceptions of nature in *King Lear.*

Danson, Lawrence, ed. *On "King Lear."* Princeton: Princeton University Press.
    Contains eight superb essays from various points of view, including Tho-
    mas Roche on tragic knowledge in *King Lear.*

Foakes, R. A. *Hamlet versus Lear: Cultural Politics and Shakespeare's Art.*
    Cambridge: Cambridge University Press, 1993. Compares Shakespeare's
    two greatest tragedies and analyzes the relevant criticism.

Halio, Jay L., ed. *Critical Essays on Shakespeare's "King Lear."* New York:
    G. K. Hall, 1996. Contains a variety of essays on Shakespeare's text,
    critical approaches, and the play in performance.

Hoeniger, F. David. *Medicine and Shakespeare in the English Renaissance.*
    Newark: University of Delaware Press, 1992. Concludes with a discus-
    sion on the development of Lear's madness.

Jorgensen, Paul A. *Lear's Self-Discovery.* Berkeley and Los Angeles: University
    of California Press, 1967. Discusses the theme of self-discovery, not only
    in the play but its meaning in the Renaissance.

Kott, Jan. *Shakespeare Our Contemporary.* Trans. Boleslow Taborski. Garden
    City, N.Y.: Doubleday Anchor, 1966. The essay, "*King Lear* and *End-
    game,*" provides an existentialist interpretation from the viewpoint of a
    middle European survivor of World War II.

Lawlor, John. *The Tragic Sense in Shakespeare.* London: Chatto and Windus,
    1969. Discusses the conflict between imaginative sympathy and the idea
    of justice in *King Lear.*

Leggatt, Alexander. *King Lear.* New York: Harvester, 1988. An excellent critical
    analysis of the play.

Mack, Maynard. *"King Lear" in Our Time.* Berkeley and Los Angeles: Uni-
    versity of California Press, 1965. One of the best, comprehensive, and

concise treatments of the play, including Shakespeare's use of his sources.

McAlindon, T. *Shakespeare's Tragic Cosmos*. Cambridge: Cambridge University Press, 1991. Begins with a theoretical discussion and medieval concepts of tragedy and proceeds to Shakespeare's major tragedies.

Nevo, Ruth. *Tragic form in Shakespeare*. Princeton: Princeton University Press, 1972. An excellent chapter on *King Lear*.

Ornstein, Robert. *The Moral Vision of Jacobean Tragedy*. Madison: University of Wisconsin Press, 1965. Contains a dozen perceptive pages on *King Lear*.

Ryan, Kiernan, ed. *King Lear*. New York: St. Martin's Press, 1992. One of the "New Casebooks" series of essays from various points of view, including cultural materialism, or Marxism.

Soellner, Rolf. *Shakespeare's Patterns of Self-Knowledge*. Columbus: Ohio State University Press, 1972. Two fine chapters on *King Lear*: "Valuing the Self" and "Stripping the Self."

Wells, Stanley. *Shakespeare: A Life in Drama*. New York: W. W. Norton, 1995. A complete survey of Shakespeare's life and work.

Whitaker, Virgil. *The Mirror Up to Nature: The Technique of Shakespeare's Tragedies*. San Marino, Calif.: Huntington Library, 1965. Notes how Shakespeare learned from *Hamlet* to separate the roles of scourge and minister in *King Lear*.

PSYCHOANALYTICAL, GENDER, AND OTHER CRITICAL APPROACHES

Battenhouse, Roy. *Shakespearean Tragedy: Its Art and Christian Premises*. Bloomington: Indiana University Press, 1969. Interprets *King Lear* from a Christian point of view.

Blechner, Mark. "King Lear, King Leir, and Incest Wishes," in *American Imago* 45 (1988): 309–25. Updates Pauncz's article (see below) on the incest theme.

Boose, Lynda. "The Father of the Bride," in *PMLA* 97 (1982): 325–47; adapted and reprinted in *Shakespeare's Middle Tragedies*, ed. David Young. Englewood Cliffs, N.J.: Prentice Hall, 1993, 207–20. On the marriage ceremony and rituals of separation.

Cavell, Stanley. *Disowning Knowledge in Six Plays of Shakespeare*. Cambridge: Cambridge University Press, 1987. Contains a long essay on *King Lear*: "The Avoidance of Love."

Doran, Madeleine. *Shakespeare's Dramatic Language*. Madison: University of Wisconsin Press, 1976. Analyzes the linguistic patterns in *King Lear*, especially the use of imperatives, interrogatives, and assertions.

Dusinberre, Juliet. *Shakespeare and the Nature of Women*. 2nd ed. New York: St. Martin's Press, 1996. Originally published twenty years earlier, this is one of the pioneering works of feminist criticism. Same text, but with a new introduction.

Erickson, Peter. *Patriarchal Structures in Shakespeare's Drama*. Berkeley and Los Angeles: University of California Press, 1985. Includes a chapter on "Maternal Images and Male Bonds in *Hamlet, Othello*, and *King Lear*."

Fortin, René. "Hermeneutical Circularity and Christian Interpretations of *King Lear*," in *Gaining upon Certainty: Selected Criticism*. Providence: Providence College Press, 1995. Tries to reconcile Christian and secular interpretations of *King Lear*, or at least show their complementary relationship.

Frye, Northrop. *Fools of Time: Studies in Shakespearean Tragedy*. Toronto: University of Toronto Press, 1967. Frye examines the mythic aspects of *King Lear* with special reference to the myths of Christianity.

Greenblatt, Stephen. "Shakespeare and the Exorcists," in *Shakespearean Negotiations*. Berkeley: University of California Press, 1988, pp. 94–128; reprinted in *Critical Essays on Shakespeare's* King Lear, ed. Jay L. Halio. New York: G. K. Hall, 1996, pp. 88–121. A New Historicist interpretation examining Shakespeare's use of Harsnett.

Halio, Jay L. "Gloucester's Blinding," *Shakespeare Quarterly* 43 (1992): 221–23. Gloucester's blinding symbolically represents castration, from a psychoanalytical standpoint.

Hawkes, Terence. *William Shakespeare: "King Lear."* Plymouth, England: Northcote House, 1995. Approaches the play as a cultural materialist.

Heilman, Robert Bechtold. *This Great Stage: Image and Structure in "King Lear."* Seattle: University of Washington Press, 1963; reprint Greenwood Press, 1976. Analyzes the imagery in connection with the thematic patterns in the play.

Holland, Norman. *Psychoanalysis and Shakespeare*. New York: McGraw-Hill, 1966. Freudian based, but still one of the best introductions to this approach to Shakespeare.

Kahn, Coppélia. "The Absent Mother in 'King Lear'," in *Rewriting the Renaissance*, ed. Margaret Ferguson, Maureen Quilligan, and Nancy Vickers. Chicago: University of Chicago Press, 1986, pp. 33–49; reprinted in *New Casebooks: King Lear*, ed. Kiernan Ryan (New York: St. Martin's Press, 1992), pp. 92–113. Family relationships and gender were important to Shakespeare, as in *King Lear*.

Lenz, Carolyn Ruth Swift, Gayle Greene, and Carol Thomas Neely, eds. *The Woman's Part: Feminist Criticism of Shakespeare*. Urbana: University of Illinois Press, 1980. Although no essay devotes itself exclusively to *King Lear* in this collection, references to the play abound in many of the articles.

McLuskie, Kate. "The Patriarchal Bard: Feminist Criticism and Shakespeare: *King Lear* and *Measure for Measure*," in *Political Shakespeare*, ed. Jonathan Dollimore and Alan Sinfield. Ithaca: Cornell University Press, 1985, pp. 88–108. On patriarchy in *King Lear*.

Pauncz, Arpad, "Psychopathology of Shakespeare's 'King Lear'," *American Imago* 9 (1952): 57–78. On the incest theme.

Rabkin, Norman. *Shakespeare and the Common Understanding*. New York: Free Press, 1967. An essential critical study, approaching the plays from the point of view of "complementarity," or the way the plays hold opposing attitudes and concepts of the meaning of life in a single harmonious vision.

KING LEAR IN PERFORMANCE

Abrams, Richard. "The Double Casting of Cordelia and Lear's Fool: A Theatrical View," *Texas Studies in Literature and Language* 27 (1985): 354–68. Disagrees with Ringler's argument (see below).

Bratton, J. S. ed., *King Lear* (Plays in Performance) (Bristol: Bristol Classical Plays, 1987. Using the Globe text on facing pages, Bratton records the ways passages and whole scenes were performed.

Halio, Jay L. and Hugh Richmond. *Shakespearean Illuminations: Essays in Honor of Marvin Rosenberg*. Newark: University of Delaware Press, 1998. Includes essays by the editors on staging *King Lear* and one by Zdenek Stribrny on *King Lear* versus *Hamlet* in Eastern Europe.

Hogan, Charles B. *Shakespeare in the Theatre: 1701–1800*. 2 vols. Oxford: Clarendon Press, 1952–57. A standard survey of eighteenth-century productions of Shakespeare.

Ioppolo, Grace. *Shakespeare Performed: Essays in Honor of R. A. Foakes*. Newark: University of Delaware Press, 2000. Contains two essays on *King Lear* and many other references.

Jackson, Russell, and Robert Smallwood, eds. *Players of Shakespeare 2*. Cambridge: Cambridge University Press, 1988. Contains an essay by Antony Sher on playing the Fool.

Leggatt, Alexander. *Shakespeare in Performance: "King Lear."* Manchester: Manchester University Press, 1991. Detailed analysis of several major modern productions, including films.

Lusardi, James, and June Schlueter. *Reading Shakespeare in Performance: "King Lear."* Rutherford, N.J.: Fairleigh Dickinson University Press, 1991. Especially good on the Granada TV version with Olivier.

Odell, George C. D. *Shakespeare from Betterton to Irving*. 2 vols. New York: Scribner's, 1920. Contains much useful information on productions and actors for the period covered.

Potter, Lois, and Arthur F. Kinney. *Shakespeare: Text and Theater: Essays in Honor of Jay L. Halio.* Newark: University of Delaware Press, 1999. A large variety of essay topics, including Alexander Leggatt's "Two Lears: Notes for an Actor."

Ringler, William A. Jr., "Shakespeare and His Actors: Some Remarks on *King Lear*," in *Shakespeare's Art from a Comparative Perspective*, ed. Wendell M. Aycock (1981), pp. 187–93. Argues that, not Armin, but a boy actor played the roles of both Cordelia and the Fool.

Rosenberg, Marvin. *The Masks of King Lear.* 1972; reprint, Newark: University of Delaware Press, 1992. An excellent, detailed compendium of theatrical interpretations, including Rosenberg's own, to about 1970.

Rothwell, Kenneth S. *A History of Shakespeare on Screen: A Century of Film and Television.* Cambridge: Cambridge University Press, 1999. The most up-to-date history of the subject.

Speaight, Robert. *Shakespeare on the Stage: An Illustrated History of Shakespearian Performance.* Boston: Little, Brown, 1973. Covers many different performances, including a number of European ones, with elaborate illustrations.

Index

About the Author

JAY L. HALIO is Professor of English at the University of Delaware. He edited the volume on *King Lear* for the New Cambridge Shakespeare series (1992), and *The First Quarto of* King Lear (1994). He has published numerous articles and several other books, including Romeo and Juliet: *A Guide to the Play* (1998), and *Understanding* The Merchant of Venice (2000), both available from Greenwood Press.